THE CAREER CARTOONIST

Other Books by Dick Gautier

The Art of Caricature
The Creative Cartoonist

THE CAREER CARTOONIST

A Step-by-Step Guide to Presenting and Selling Your Artwork

DICK GAUTIER

A Perigee Book

To Pam

A Perigee Book
Published by The Berkley Publishing Group
200 Madison Avenue
New York, NY 10016

First Perigee edition: July 1992

The Putnam Berkley World Wide Web site address is
http://www.berkley.com

Library of Congress Cataloging-in-Publication Data

Gautier, Dick.
    The career cartoonist: a step-by-step guide to presenting and
selling your artwork / Dick Gautier.
        p.   cm.
    "A Perigee book."
    Includes bibliographical references and index.
    ISBN 0-399-51732-4 (alk. paper)
    1. Cartooning—Technique. 2. Caricatures and cartoons—Marketing.
3. Publicity. I. Title.
    NC1320.G37   1992   92-1024 CIP
    741.5—dc20

Cover design by Bob Silverman
Cover art © by Dick Gautier

Printed in the United States of America
5   6   7   8   9   10

This book is printed on acid-free paper.

Acknowledgments

I'd like to extend my deepest appreciation to the following people, without whom . . . Well, who knows how this all would've turned out.

Ginger Marino Miller, my very helpful editor
Tom Braccato of Hanna-Barbera Productions
Jim Cavett of Tribune Media Services
Kevin Dwinnell of Hanna-Barbera
Evelyne and Bud Johnson
Larry Le Francis of Klasky-Csupo
Kathy O'Reilly of Recycled Paper Products
Mary C. Sugett of Universal Press Syndicate
Joseph Szabo of Witty World

and all the cartoonists, caricaturists, illustrators, animators . . . let's just cut through all this and say "artists" . . . who graciously allowed me to use their words and their work in this book. Without their kindness, cooperation and generosity, this book would be a pale thing indeed. I thank you all most sincerely.

The author gratefully acknowledges permission from the following sources to reprint material in their control.

Kathie Abrams, for illustrations on pages 28 (© Kathie Abrams 1982), 36 ("Celebrate" © Kathie Abrams 1985 and "Daughters of Chutzpah" © Kathie Abrams 1984), 37 (© Kathie Abrams 1988), 89 (Illustrations © Kathie Abrams 1983: from *It's Not Fair* by Susie Hoch Morgenstern; Farrar, Straus & Giroux and © Kathie Abrams 1983: from *Goats Are Better Than Worms* by Kathleen Thomas; Dodd, Mead & Company), and 98.

Andrews and McMeel and Universal Press Syndicate, for Oz cards on pages 93 (© 1986 The Far Side by Gary Larson), 95 (© 1991 Giffin and Overmyer and © 1985 D. Noel), 97 (both © 1991 Kevin Whitlark), 101 (© 1991 Cook and Skelton), 104 (© 1988 The Far Side by Gary Larson), and 105 (© 1989 Britt and Coleman).
All Rights Reserved.

Brian Ajhar, for illustrations on pages 38, 39, 40, and 87.

Robert Camargo, for illustration on page 113.

Cartoonists & Writers Syndicate and Kevin Kallaugher, for illustrations on pages 81 and 82 (KAL, *The Baltimore Sun,* © 1991 Cartoonists & Writers Syndicate).

Cartoonists & Writers Syndicate and Jerry Robinson, for illustrations on pages 83 and 84 (© 1991 Jerry Robinson, Cartoonists & Writers Syndicate).

Eldon C. Doty, for illustrations on pages 21, 41, 42, and 43.

Mary Grace Eubank, for illustrations on pages 29, 44, 88, and 94.

Evelyne Johnson Associates, for illustrations on pages 85 and 87 (both by Frank Daniel), 86 (by Larry Daste), 90 (by Cathy Beylon and by John O'Brien).

Lance Falk, for illustration on page 109.

Michael Fleishman, for illustrations on pages 44, 45, and 46 (all © Michael Carl Fleishman).

Gerry Gersten, for illustrations on pages 47 and 48.

Hanna-Barbera Productions, for "The Hanna-Barbera Traditional Animation Process Starring Yogi Bear®" on pages 110 and 111 (© 1991 Hanna-Barbera Productions, Inc.). All Rights Reserved.

Art Leonardi, for illustrations on pages 113 and 114.

Benton Mahan, for illustrations on pages 49, 53, and 89 (source for both: *One-Minute Favorite Fairy Tales* by Shari Lewis, illustrations © 1985 by Doubleday & Company, Inc.)

Jimmy Margulies, for the illustration on page 80 (© Jimmy Margulies, *The Record*, NJ).

Jeff Moores, for illustrations on page 50.

MTV Networks, for illustrations on pages 115 and 116 (Rugrats characters courtesy of Nickelodeon TM & © 1991 MTV Networks). All Rights Reserved.

Steve Phillips, for illustrations on pages 51, 52, 60, and 61 (all © Steve Phillips, source: Landmark Calendars); and for greeting cards on pages 94, 100, 101, and 103 (all © Steve Phillips, source: Recycled Paper Products, Inc.).

Recycled Paper Products, Inc., for greeting cards on pages 91, 96, and 100 (all original designs by The Dales, © RPP, Inc.); and for greeting cards on pages 98, 99, and 104 (all original designs by Sandra Boynton, © RPP, Inc.).

Tribune Media Services, for illustrations on pages 58, 59, and 60 (all Charlie by Rodrigues); 59 (by Moore); 77 (by Jeff MacNelly, *Chicago Tribune*); 78 (by Steve Benson, © *Morning News Tribune*, Tacoma); and 79 (both by Steve Benson, © *Arizona Republic*).

Universal Press Syndicate, for comic strips on pages 65 (Calvin and Hobbes by Bill Watterson), 66 (Fox Trot by Bill Amend), 70 (Adam® by Brian Basset) and 74 (cathy® by Cathy Guisewite).

WittyWorld International Cartoon Magazine, for illustrations from their files on pages 34 (© Dragan Bosnić/Yugoslavia), 55 (© Borislav Stankovič/Yugoslavia and © Bob Vincke/Belgium), 59 (© Joe Szabo/USA), 62 (© Turhan Selcuk/Turkey), 63 (© Bob Darroch/New Zealand), and 64 (© Fontanarrosa/Argentina).

Contents

As I was saying . . . The reason I begin this way is that I feel as though I'm now picking up where I left off in my last book, *The Creative Cartoonist*. I wanted to add so much to that book, but unfortunately I didn't have the time or the space to do so. So, I simply had to write *this* book to "drop the other shoe." Plus, I received so many letters from budding artists who naturally wanted to know "Okay, what now?" "Where do I go?" "How do I get into the marketplace?" that I felt compelled to write this follow-up to try to answer some of those questions. Besides, things were slow and I like to keep busy.

I'm aiming this book at the more advanced artist, the person who can draw and create but doesn't know exactly how to proceed from that point on. I'll try to tackle a few problems that more accomplished cartoonists occasionally have, such as blocks (or ruts, if you will) where they find themselves creating the same character or characters over and over again, thus limiting their horizons in the workplace. I'll show you ways to climb out of those ruts in the chapter entitled "Breakout."

We'll address the issue of agents—if you need them and how to get them. I'll tell you how to prepare a portfolio that will attract some prospective agents or buyers, and I'll discuss panel cartoons, comic strips, greeting cards, children's books, the animation field and the realities of seeking employment in those marketplaces. I'll reveal more advanced techniques needed to compete in the area of illustration and the tools required. I'll give you sources of current prospective markets, tell you how to contact the potential buyers and how to best present your wares. I'll quote leading illustrators/cartoonists from all over the country and I'll also interview a few friends and acquaintances who work professionally in these areas so they can provide a keener insight into their specific areas of endeavor.

And don't listen to the naysayers, those out there who continue to see cartooning as a dying art. All the arts are fragile; they go through booms and busts like any other career (save the mortuary business and maybe VCR repair). Lee Lorenz, the art director of *The New Yorker* magazine and an extremely talented artist, recently stated: "I don't think cartooning is a dying art, just on the strength of the young people coming into it. I think there are a lot of possibilities for people who are as sensitive and creative as the coming generation of cartoonists. They'll definitely continue to express their talent—whether they'll do it in magazines or somewhere else. I don't know, but I don't feel we're at the end. You have a problem when you're running out of talent, and I don't think there's any sign of that."

Encouraging words from a pro who has successfully toiled in the cartoon industry for several decades; he believes that the future of cartooning is only as bright as the newcomers in the marketplace. . . . So let's go to work.

I'm going to deal with as many aspects of cartooning as a career as I can (it is a career but for the purposes of this book I'm going to treat it more like a business). The ins, the outs, the ups, the downs, the pluses and minuses . . . portfolios and panels, agents and animation, cards and comics, materials and markets and, of course, drafting, doodling and downright dumb drawings. (I apologize for that outburst. . . . I've got to get over this unnatural fondness for alliteration.)

AREER

Cartooning as a career actually has some distinct advantages. For one thing, many of the working cartoonists have no formal schooling in art, so that should be encouraging news to some of you. That doesn't mean, however, that if you have the finances, the time and the opportunity to attend school or classes you shouldn't go. There's nothing that you couldn't learn on your own, given enough time, but who wants to spend that much time at it when art schools are wonderful shortcuts (it becomes the "infinite number of monkeys" concept). It's better to go to school if you can. However, I feel that in this book I'm addressing many who are unable to do so.

I think that cartooning is probably one of the best part-time and least expensive careers that you can embark upon. The investment can be quite low (we'll tackle the subject of materials in the next chapter), and it can all be accomplished right from your studio, kitchen, or wherever you choose (or are forced) to work. Do the work and leave the rest to the U.S. Postal Service and AT&T.

I hear grumblings and rumblings now and then about the state of the art of cartooning. And make no mistake about it, it is an art. Ed Sorel, one of the truly brilliant artists, regards cartooning as "a higher calling than illustration, but in my heart of hearts, I am an illustrator who does cartoons . . . cartoons are a reflection of the head doing the art, while illustrating is a reflection of the skills of the person doing the art."

Of course it's true that there are now fewer markets for the panel cartoon, but animation is a reawakened and thriving industry, and things like animatronics, which we'll touch on briefly later, are supplying other venues for the cartoonist's work *and* there are spot drawings and wrapping papers and greeting cards and humor books and so on . . . and so on . . .

Cartooning resembles acting as a career since both have sporadic, unpredictable natures. Hollywood waiters and waitresses are almost always waiting for their break in movies. (A comedy on Broadway has a scene in a restaurant where the customer, to get the waitress's attention, calls out, "Oh, actress!") Cartoonists, too, wait for their first big break. You can stay holed up in your room and turn out brilliant cartoons and send them off and wait . . . and wait. Waiting is something for which you're going to have to develop an aptitude. Also, both careers can be done in your spare time . . . to begin with, anyway. You can go to school or hang in with a nine-to-five job and still peddle your wares out there in the marketplace.

Do you notice how I'm subtly but systematically removing all the cop-outs, excuses and alibis from your path so that you'll be forced to become a cartoonist?

I'm just trying to forewarn and thereby forearm you with the truth about this business. There is stiff competition out there but that doesn't mean you can't beat the odds and succeed. To do so requires hard work, dedication, application, perseverance and some sacrifice. If you choose to pursue this career, you might have to give up a few luxuries . . . little things like food and shelter and clothing. I'm jesting, of course (a bit). However, it's worth remembering that, as Chuck Jones wryly states in *Chuck Amuck,* his delightful autobiography: "Creativity always thrives in opposition . . . when you take yourself seriously you're dead."

You'll have to learn to exercise willpower . . . or maybe I should say "won't power." "I won't go to the movies tonight, I'll stay home and draw instead." That's what's really of primary importance here. Application. Don't procrastinate. Draw. Sketch. Doodle. Constantly. Obsessively. Wherever you go, take your sketch pad with you and "steal" faces and body language from wherever human beings congregate . . . restaurants, parks, ball games, wherever. I love to sketch in public; throughout the following (and a few preceding) pages I've included a few sketches of people that I've "stolen" from airports, restaurants or wherever I happened to be.

The best inspiration, of course, always lies in life, but there are always other alternatives, like magazines, books, museums and wherever else the human form is seen. Or use the zoo for a fresh approach, a little reverse anthropomorphism; that is, imbue the human face with bestial qualities and come up with something totally different.

I would suggest that right now you should start to assemble a picture file (still known fondly to some as a "morgue"), which is a collection of clippings of everything and anything gathered from books, newspapers, magazines, ads, circulars, whatever. Whenever you spot an interesting face or figure—an athlete in action, a candid photo from the front page or some paparazzi's shot from one of the tabloids that grace our supermarket checkout stands—clip it out and file it away.

Browse through old magazine shops (I do. They smell funny but it's worth it). Find pictures of room interiors (upscale and seedy), cars, planes, people roller-skating, walking on the beach . . . The list is endless but it'll all be used. Trust me.

Organize your clippings alphabetically, cross-reference if you wish, but do it, you'll find it to be an indispensable aid in your work. I'm sure you've experienced that awful frustration when you're looking for a picture of a certain item—an X-ray machine, a tractor or some other odd-looking piece of equipment that you just can't remember what the heck it looks like. If you've run across a picture of it before and filed it under HOSPITALS or FARMS, it'll be there waiting for you. Here are some suggestions for categories, but please feel free to find your own system. In fact I encourage you to do so. . . . You'll be able to find your stuff easier.

Airports (including planes and equipment)

Anatomy (bones, muscles and stuff)

Animals (exotic ones and pets . . . everything)

Appliances (washing machines, refrigerators, toasters, coffee makers)

Architecture (interiors, exteriors, foreign and domestic)

Automobiles (all sizes, shapes and styles)

Cities (from Natchez to New York to Nairobi . . . sorry about that!)

Costumes (foreign, historical, domestic . . . including uniforms)

Electronics (computers, stereos, CDs, VCRs)

Farming (machines, buildings, etc.)

Figures (people of all ages in action and at rest, at work and at play)

Foods (all kinds from all lands)

Furniture

Greenery (lawns, flowers, bushes, shrubs, trees)

Guns (handguns to rifles)

Heads (close-ups of men, women and children, famous and unknown)

Holidays (Christmas to Saint Swithin's Day, with all the appropriate symbols; weddings and celebrations)

Landscapes (scenes beautiful, ravaged and otherwise)

Music (instruments, notations, conductors)

Prints (floral designs, checks, plaids, etc.)

Schools (buildings and materials)

Sci-fi

Sports (athletic equipment of every variety)

Textures (leathers, velvets, laces, brick, etc.)

Theater (opera, ballet, film, the circus; all-inclusive)

Tools

Toys (dolls, stuffed animals, etc.)

Trains

War (tanks, heavy artillery, missiles)

Water (oceans, seas, ponds, rivers, ice, sleet, snow)

I believe in warming up before you begin to draw. Much like a runner stretching his muscles or a pitcher tossing some easy overhands, I think that as an artist you have to constantly reacquaint your hand with the pen and paper . . . especially if you're given to hatch or crosshatch techniques, which require finely tuned coordination. So, grab a piece of paper and your pen or pencil and do a few loosening-up exercises.

First, make swirls, parallel lines, crosshatches and loops and practice with one line thinning or thickening as you go. Draw faces and figures in an unbroken line without removing your pen from the paper—a great loosening-up exercise. You have to be free because you're preparing for the task at hand—drawing funny pictures to sell to people. (Sounds weird but that's what it is, isn't it?)

Then begin to draw, not restrictedly and cautiously but freely and with abandon. Remember that these scribblings are not going to be exhibited or saved; no one will see them, so enjoy it. When you're finished and you look at what you've done, it'll probably be the best work of your life. Try it.

Get together with some friends who draw, and take turns posing for each other. But when I say posing I mean holding some object in a quickly assumed pose for ten, maybe twenty seconds tops, while the others try to capture the essence of that moment. Did you capture the weight of the body, the way one leg handled all the weight, the bored facial expression? In twenty seconds? Impossible, you say? Maybe, but you will loosen up your approach to the art of cartooning. Because that's what it's about—capturing something in as few lines as possible with as much humor as possible. Look at the great cartoonists, look at the working ones; they're easy and confident. The name of the game is "casual." Why do you think so many cartoonists draw the same figure repeatedly, using tracing paper? To get it to look less contrived, less cautiously thought out. That's an aspect of the art of cartooning that you should aspire to, because once you learn that, you can always pull back and produce more controlled works. But first you have to learn to let the pendulum swing wide in that other, freer direction.

# ATERIALS

All right, shall we discuss materials? If you already have them, know what you like and are comfortable with them, you may want to rush on to the next section. When it comes to materials the choices available to you are as varied as the stars themselves. I'm sure you've done some experimenting already. Perhaps you prefer pen, pencil, pastels, papers or parchments for your protean picturizations . . . (sorry, I'm having a minor attack here!) . . . Anyway, you get the idea. Narrow your sights and it'll cost you a lot less. Be honest with yourself and determine which is your forte, then go for that one. Some artists simply don't gravitate toward pen-and-ink. No big deal—stick with pencil or whatever makes you comfortable and helps you to produce your best work. Or, like Brian Ajhar, whom we'll discuss in a later chapter on illustration, you might want to creatively mix your media.

Pens run the gamut from the old-fashioned dip-in-ink variety to the sophisticated mechanical pens with the replaceable cartridges. And every artist will extol the merits of the particular pen that he or she loves. It comes down to this: Try them out, find the one that gives the best results and stick with it. Ed Sorel, one of the finest practitioners of this unusual art of cartooning, uses a Hunt Globe Bowl pen but it's not for everyone. Pens' differences lie primarily in their flexibility—how they respond to the pressure of your hand to yield a thinner or thicker line. On the other hand, felt-tips (which a lot of artists swear by) have almost no give so the line remains fairly constant. I'd suggest going to your favorite art store and trying out a few right there before committing to them. Try these for size and feeling: Hunt #99, the Hunt Globe Bowl, of which we spoke, an Extra Fine Bowl Point #512 and, of course, don't forget the line of good old standby Speedball pens with the wide range of replaceable nibs. There are four basic shapes in the Speedball line: the A is square, B round, C oblong and D oval. The 0 is the largest while the 6 is the smallest. Speedballs, like felt-tips, produce a consistent line with little variation. I'd recommend getting a small selection to begin with: a couple of intermediate Cs, like 3 or 4, and a few Bs. The A5 gives you a fine line for scratchy techniques (you can use a crow quill along with it to great effect). A technique that I've always been fond of is using a Flair felt-tip and then wetting my finger slightly in order to smear the ink. I like the look and feel of it and you'll find it's very controllable.

The mechanical pens also produce uniform widths. Radiographs go from 0 to 6, which is the widest line; the advantage is that your flow is not interrupted by constant dipping. Then there are fountain pens, which have more line variance because of their flexibility. Try out an Osmiroid, a Pelikan, Esterbrook or the Mont Blanc; they're all fine pens. I like to use a variety of Penstix, which range from F (for Fine) to EEF (Extra-Extra Fine). I just use them and toss them away. Nothing to clean up or refill but then sometimes I feel a little lackluster, lazy and lethargic (I know . . . I know . . . I'll back off) on occasion. Anyway go and try them before you invest and you'll be pleased that you did. I did a lot of the work in this book with Penstix.

The pencil is my favorite implement because I like the subtleties that it allows. I like to shade and smear and erase for highlights . . . I just like pencils. Again, you have many choices: a 2B to 6B is extremely responsive; it doesn't require much pressure, it's encouraging and easy. If you're of a mind to work in a more precise manner, go for a harder lead, up in the range of 2H to 6H, but only if you're going to be more exact and not as loose. It's a good idea to buy a variety of pencils and draw the same thing over again with each one to see what feels best. It is, after all the intellectualizing about widths, softness, hardness, etc., still a totally subjective decision. How does it "feel" to you? I like Wolff's carbon pencils, charcoal sticks and especially grease pencils, which are a favorite of political and sports cartoonists.

Here are a couple of sketches (including a rather morose self-portrait) in which I drew out the basic shape in ink and then shaded it in grease pencil. Try this technique for some interesting effects and good control.

The surface upon which you draw is just as important as the implement you use, helping to dictate the final result. The surfaces are, simplistically speaking, light, heavy, smooth or rough. These textures in combination with various tools can produce an incredibly wide spectrum of techniques. Plate finishes, bristols and vellums have a slippery surface, which is ideal for pen-and-ink work, while more textured papers like watercolor papers, Strathmore and charcoal papers respond much better to pencil since they have a "tooth." Some artists like papers with a woolly surface while others prefer pebbly papers that cause the lines to skip in a random manner, thus producing a looser, less controlled effect.

And here are a couple of sketches on rough napkins.

But paper can be expensive, especially if you're given to lots of preliminary sketching, so I'd recommend getting a batch of newsprint (cheap by paper standards) or some Aquabee all-purpose paper. I like to work, as I've discovered many of my compatriots do, with Professional Parchment tracing paper; that way I can rework a drawing (without the use of a light board) until it's done to my satisfaction. However, the prior advice is sound only if you're not planning on working with wash. In *that* case a whole new set of standards present themselves since you'll have to deal with the dreaded "curling" syndrome. To avoid the curling, use smoother bonds and bristols or even regular typing paper, as long as you get the twenty-pound bond; or mount the thinner paper on board before you apply your wash. But again, visit your art store, nose around, ask around and experiment. A good, rule-of-thumb guide regarding paper consists of the following:

Bristols are postcard weight and heavier. They're good for ink and they take erasing well. They won't curl under wash.

Vellum has a semi-smooth surface and also comes in a transparent sheet. It is good for drawing, ink or wash.

Charcoal is coarse with a good tooth. It's recommended for pencil, and ink if you want the line to "stutter."

Coated papers are extremely smooth and come in many colors and weights. They're good for ink, pencil and markers, and they take wash quite well.

Construction is very absorbent and rough. It is a fibrous paper that comes in a variety of colors.

Newsprint and Bonds are good for sketching and layout. Bond is also fine for some finish work but the thinner ones curl up with wash.

Brushes, as compared to pens, are more casual, not as constricted and controlled. Yet there are pens in the hands of masterful artists like David Levine that flow and weave with a divine looseness unrivaled by most brush users. So ultimately it's in your hands.

Now, there are brushes and then there are brushes. Sable holds its point better than the man-made variety but they are quite expensive. You can buy sable on the low end, as opposed to the high end, and save yourself a considerable amount of money, but I would recommend investing in a few good ones if you can, probably a #2, #1 and a #6 will do for starters.

Inks are also a subjective choice, but for all-around work, a couple of bottles of Higgins, Pelikan, Koh-i-noor or Artone would be good. Waterproof inks should be used under washes or colored ink work. Special inks are available for mechanical pens and fountain pens. That list is available where you purchase the pens.

White-out, a bleedproof opaque paint, is an indispensable commodity for rectifying minor slips of the pen or brush. You might also consider investing in a pencil sharpener, the old-fashioned hand-crank variety that allows you to sharpen any size pencil, not the battery-operated variety with one size hole.

You'll also need a cutting tool like an X-acto knife, a Pink Pearl eraser and a gum eraser, some cotton balls for shading charcoal, masking tape and tubes of rubber cement. The rubber cement will be used for a technique known as "quilting," which I'll discuss in a later chapter. Rubber cement also acts as a protective film for sections of your drawing that you want untouched. You can paint and draw and when you're done, merely rub the cement into a ball and voilà! The original drawing is undisturbed. It's also fun to peel off (shades of sunburn aftermath).

It's a good idea to have a blue, nonphoto pencil on hand for sketching; that way you won't have to erase lines . . . unless you're painting over the sketch; then it's necessary to clean it up well. And to risk sounding parental . . . clean up your materials; it'll save you a lot of money. Good sable brushes, if properly cared for, rinsed out and put away after use, can last a long time; but allow the ink to dry on them when you get a last-minute call to go to dinner with a friend and you'll be replacing them sooner than you'd like.

And it's wise to purchase half a dozen cheap white cotton gloves. I wear one on my drawing hand (I look sort of like a second-string Michael Jackson) so that I don't constantly smudge and smear my work. They're highly absorbent and they'll save you a lot of cleanup down the road. Wear them for ink or pencil work. Wash them often, as the materials do tend to accumulate in them.

I've already mentioned a light box, which is basically a wooden shell covered by a piece of glass with a light underneath, used for tracing purposes. You can either build your own, if you've a gift for carpentry, or you can purchase a very deep picture frame (deep enough to accommodate a light bulb or a row of fluorescent bulbs safely), about 18″ × 24″, and place the lights underneath and trace on the glass on top. I'd recommend against using plastic or Lucite for the top. It doesn't take kindly to knives and sharp pencils, and it has a tendency to bow. Use clear glass, since frosted is more expensive and doesn't work any better. Keep the corners of your light box square so it can be used with your measuring instruments like a triangle or a T square. For a very small investment you'll have a piece of equipment that will pay you back again and again.

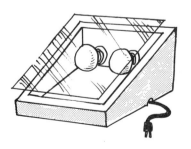

For those of you who are able to afford airbrush equipment, I would most heartily recommend that investment. It is, when mastered, one of those techniques that take cartooning out of one level and elevate it (according to some of the powers-that-be) into the realm of "illustration." It is true that when you redo the simplest cartoon design with airbrush, it suddenly and inexplicably takes on more significance and import. Airbrushes are basically little pumps with an extremely fine hole so that you can mist an area or cover it completely but evenly.

There are conventional airbrushes and marker airbrushes (those that attach directly to a marker). The disadvantages of the latter are that once they are used up you have to switch to another marker, and also you have no choice in colors but what's available in the markers, no custom paint mixing. But as you learn to use the airbrush, which is controlled by a small valve—press down and the air is released, pull toward you and the ink is released—you'll be stimulated by its wide range of uses. Airbrushing sounds incredibly simple but it does take lots of paper, many cups of ink and hours of patience to develop the subtle touch needed to master this technique.

If you're going to be doing only a small area at a time, you can hook up to the aerosol cans that are made for this purpose, instead of the costly generator or the turbine-charged models. The aerosol cans should provide you with about three hours of working time. Also, since the airbrush is an instrument that requires constant attention and thorough cleanup, it's recommended that you run water through it after each use to prevent clogging. And a word of warning: The constant inhaling of these fumes could have an injurious effect on your lungs so you should wear a respirator.

You'll also have to learn how to "mask off" an area. This is accomplished in a variety of ways: cutting out the area to be airbrushed with an X-acto knife, using masking tape or simple bond paper, or covering the area with a glutinous substance known as liquid frisket, which peels off quite easily when dry. I prefer using frisket.

On the next page is a fine example of the airbrush technique in "Mechanical Bird" by Eldon C. Doty, a successful and, as you can see, very humorous illustrative cartoonist. There's more of his work to be seen in later chapters, but you can see how skillfully he wields his airbrush while still managing to maintain a casual feel and a sense of humor.

There's a very inexpensive version of the airbrush that I've used successfully for years. All you need is to mask off an area and get an old toothbrush and some ink. I dip the brush in the ink and run my thumb along it, flicking it and spraying it as I go. You can achieve very interesting effects with this cheap imitation.

A movable lamp is another item that every artist should eventually add to his or her list. There's no substitute for good lighting.

A few artists of my acquaintance have elaborate work areas with lots of fancy drawing tables, lights and equipment, but they don't always turn out a very impressive product. It's a little like buying a ton of upscale tennis togs and high-tech rackets but if you can't hit the ball, well . . . Ilie Nastase, the tennis great, once said that the most important part of the racket is the area from the wrist up to the shoulder. The same thing applies here. The most important part of the pen is the hand guiding it. So don't get intimidated by not being able to afford the best. If you have the talent, ultimately it will shine through and overcome any lack of sophisticated materials. The good news is that it isn't necessary to lay out a lot of cash initially. A few pencils, some pens, ink, whites, a pad of paper, some envelopes and stamps and you're in business. The rest is up to you.

BREAKOUT

This chapter is entitled "Breakout" because that's how I perceive freeing yourself from the restrictions of sameness. The ability to break down behavioral patterns that have limited your artistic vision and abilities will allow you to move into a more creative realm. This chapter is directed primarily toward those of you out there who have fallen into that rut of drawing the same character or face over and over again, and you just can't seem to get beyond it. I believe there's a simple way to climb out of that hole that involves playing with spatial relationships. After all, isn't that what drawing, and especially cartooning, is in the first place?

First you'll have to desert some nasty little habits in order to broaden your scope. The creation of original characters is a necessary skill in the cartoonist's bag of tricks. If you have difficulty in coming up with that new twist on a face there are, I believe, some exercises that can help to break down that rut or creative block.

First of all, if you usually start with the eyes, don't. If the nose is your usual beginning point, make a concerted effort to change it. Break your hand's pattern; I know it's comfortable and easy but that might be the problem. You have to shake it out of its lethargy by forcing it to behave differently. Try whatever it is you're not doing. Begin with the shape of the face or start with the ears or hair and work downward—anything to break that hand-eye coordination pattern that results in the same tired configuration. For example, do you always start with the head shape? Then don't. Instead, draw the same set of features three times and then surround each one with a different head shape . . . almost as an afterthought.

Here's an exercise that works for me when I feel myself getting stale or repetitive in my drawings. I draw that cliché face, divide it into thirds and rearrange the features within that framework or grid. I'll place the eyes down below the nose line or shove them way up where the brow is.

I know a screenwriter who writes all his scenes on 3 × 5 cards and spreads the entire movie out on his floor. Then he gathers up the cards, shuffles them and deals them in a random left-to-right pattern, thus forcing relationships and the juxtaposition of scenes that his too logical mind would never come up with. Crazy? Not really, not if it can free you up and inspire you to be better and reach higher. This is the same kind of thing. Force yourself to stretch. You might go too far sometimes but that's okay; you can always come back a little. The important thing is you've reached out for something new, you've explored creative virgin territory.

Here are some more examples. With this face I gradually made the nose larger. The eyes and mouth changed accordingly in order to fill the face space. Now, if I were to merely change the hair it would create three totally new and different characters.

Here's a profile with a few options sketched in as to how far you could go with his mouth, nose and chin. Consider it a game and use whatever inspiration is handy.

Try out these exercises and by sticking with it and making it a daily ritual, you'll soon see yourself breaking out of that sameness syndrome.

Here I've drawn an intentionally wimpy-looking, nerdy guy, but look what happens when I just change his neck. He takes on a whole different aspect. Feel free to mix clichés; take an obvious tough-guy type and dress him differently or change his expression radically. Play, have fun, get weird, and it'll start those creative juices flowing.

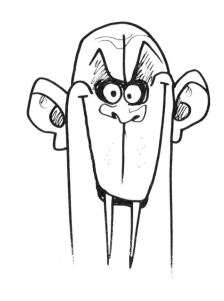

Here's a silly-looking vampire, but watch what happens when I move his nose around. It totally changes his look and each time creates a new version of the character.

Of course the best source for faces is life. Do caricatures of your family, friends, the guys on your bowling team, the women at work. It doesn't matter if there's no resemblance. A caricature is a recognizable picture of a specific individual, but if it's a bad caricature just forget the source and you've got a wonderfully new, interesting face. We do the same thing in the animated voice-over business. Do a bad impression of John Wayne or Jack Nicholson and you've created a whole new character voice. Another idea is to turn on the TV to the news, kill the sound (it's too negative anyway) and draw every face that comes on the screen. Do it quickly, grab a nose here and a head shape there. Create a combination of Willard Scott, Regis Philbin and Jane Pauley . . . anything to stir your imagination and get it cooking.

The thing is to never be satisfied with sameness. If it looks too familiar, redo it. Constantly play with those good old spatial relationships until you see a whole fresh batch of characters emerge. Have fun with this concept. I think it will be time well spent at your drawing board.

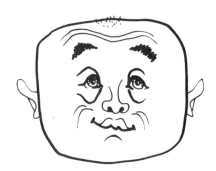

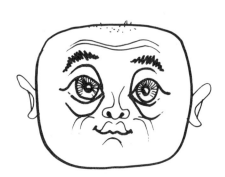

PORTFOLIO

Portfolios are basically visual résumés, a device with which to show the prospective client or agent your wares—talent on parade. The trilemma here is whether it's wisest to stress your own unique style or your versatility or both, which possesses the inherent danger of overwhelming and subsequently confusing the prospective client. The answer, insofar as I'm concerned, lies within the extent of your expertise as an all-around cartoon artist. If your style bears an unmistakably individual stamp that cannot be denied nor imitated, like the wild Don Martin from *Mad* magazine, for instance, then go with that. However, if your forte (please pronounce it *fort* and not *for-tay*) is your amazing ability to work proficiently in any and all styles and media, then that's most certainly what you should advertise.

Now, you could go out and spend enormous amounts on fancy folders and color reproductions but that's still no guarantee that the guy with the sketches on typewriter paper in the manila envelope won't take the job away from you. Presentation is important but ability is uppermost.

Kathie Abrams, a talented and busy cartoon artist, has some very definite ideas regarding portfolios. In Michael Fleishman's excellent book *Getting Started as a Freelance Illustrator or Designer,* she states that "the portfolio should stay out of the way of your art. If it quietly and efficiently showcases your work, it's doing its job." She goes on to say, "I've used a big portfolio—a museum box–type affair measuring about 16″ × 18″ and weighing a ton. I used it for two years—my back went out twice—because I really wanted to make an impression and be able to show spreads. It went over quite well but I'm happier with my 11″ × 14″ box."

Most illustrators and cartoonists agree that your portfolio should basically reflect your individual style, that is the strongest thing that you have to sell— your unique view of the world as seen through your work. Also, think of your portfolio as an entity, a story, if you will, with a beginning, a middle and an end. Choose the first piece carefully to whet their appetite and then move into something totally different and then mix it up, and so on until you produce a flow, a planned continuity that will hold the viewer's attention as your art moves from concept to concept and style to style. In other words, don't just arbitrarily stuff a mess of work in a box and call it a portfolio, because it isn't. Like the nightclub performer who does ten songs in a row with no carefully planned emotional hills and valleys, the haphazardly thrown together portfolio also fails to do its job properly.

Mary Grace Eubank, a successful humorous illustrator, says, "When I graduated from college, I had never even heard of a portfolio. I had excellent grades, but the people at my first job interview could not have cared less about honors or grades or anything. They wanted to see a portfolio, and I didn't even know what they were talking about." Obviously she learned that lesson and well. Today she doesn't change her portfolio, she merely keeps it up to date. Here's an example of her work.

Faces are important in a portfolio because they are the most expressive part of the body and emotion counts (it's what reaches out to you from an ad). When you're made to feel something by a drawing or a painting, then that artwork has power. And *that's* what creative directors or art directors are looking for. Also, you should represent a variety of subjects, such as automobiles, foods, cosmetics. Demonstrate your skills by showing groups of people involved in the

more mundane "American" activities, such as bowling or picnicking or sitting around the Thanksgiving dinner table. Think Norman Rockwell for some of your stuff; it is, after all, what you might be called upon to do by some commercial houses. Some artists opt to mat each piece but doing so makes for more bulk and weight so that's strictly a personal choice. Lamination is another way to go since it does help to prolong the life of the work. I'd recommend ten to twenty pieces as a good-sized portfolio—small enough to take up just enough of their time, yet large enough to display your versatility and range.

If you're not located in one of the main centers of activity like New York, Chicago or Los Angeles, and you choose to mail your portfolio, be sure never to send original art. Send only high-quality photocopies, Photostats or C-prints. Another option to look into is slides, easy enough for you to photograph at home if you have a fairly decent camera and purchase a heavy-duty binder (one that will travel well) with which to present your work.

Keep a thorough and neat record of what you've sent to whom and how long they've had it before building paranoid "dungeons in the air" about its being lost and convincing yourself that you'll never see it again. You can always follow up with a polite phone call after a decent interval of time has elapsed.

Most good art stores have a stock of heavy-paper portfolios that will do the job very nicely, after all you're only trying to keep your work together and neat. I think it's all you need. I would encourage you to include a few pieces of your work in color. In fact, as many techniques as you have mastered, within the context of your style, should be a part of your portfolio. Also slip in some good extra copies of some of your work so that if someone is interested you can leave them with a sample (of course with your name, address and other pertinent information stamped on the back).

Some artists make up several portfolios designed specifically for different markets but I feel that that's a lot of unnecessary trouble. Most editors worth their salt can spot good work and versatility without its being narrowed down to their specific needs. Talent is talent and ability is ability, and the portfolio should demonstrate those facts without question. Good art directors are looking for consistency and versatility; use that as your rule of thumb. But just keep in mind that well-known, time-worn axiom: "Eight great pieces are better than twenty mediocre ones."

MARKETS

The cartoon market, like any other business, goes through ups and downs and phases. It shrinks, it expands, it changes. One area will soften and then suddenly something like animatronics will emerge and bring with it more work for the cartoonist. The secret, I believe, is to become well versed and keep up to date in all the potential markets and just hammer away at them. There's no substitute for "sticktoitiveness" and self-promotion.

Before we proceed, let's discuss the pros and cons of artists' representatives ("agent" sometimes sounds like a dirty word). Whether or not you use an agent is based primarily upon you, your personality and your work habits. If you are a terrific self-starter, a disciplined person who can get up in the morning and not only do your artwork but also get on the phone or go to your typewriter, send out letters and make contacts, woo art directors with tireless energy, then maybe an agent is superfluous. If, on the other hand, you are not terribly good with people (no crime that) and you can't be bothered with all the politicking that's required to bandy your name about out there in the marketplace, then you should try to get yourself an artist's representative. Also, if you're logistically disadvantaged by being some distance from the advertising mainstream, it might be wise to use an agent who can do your legwork for you.

Most representatives take 25 to 35 percent for their efforts, which is a considerable sum, but then again you are availing yourself of their expertise and contacts. They can often open doors that very well might be closed to you under other circumstances, and they do have the ear and the confidence of the agencies. Most representatives do have a keen eye and a good sense of where to best market your particular style. You'd no doubt have to shop around for quite a while before you could consummate that perfect ménage à trois of art, style and client, whereas an agent can cut through that and save you considerable time and effort. To say that agents are a necessary evil is a way of belittling a group of men and women who provide a worthwhile service to artists. Some extremely successful illustrators come to depend upon their agents and would be lost without them. The agent has a stable of artists from which to choose, and he or she has an innate sense of who belongs where and with whom, so if a call comes in for a certain kind of work the agent can go directly to that artist and zero in on the account.

Now, how do you obtain the services of an agent and how do you make him or her aware of you as an artist? There are only a couple of avenues to explore: First, you should invest in a mailing card that has a sample of your very best work and get a list of agents from either a book like *The Writer's Yellow Pages,* an indispensable favorite of mine, or *American Illustration Showcase* (a good art store should carry it). Ferret out the names and addresses of various agents and send a batch of the cards off in shotgun fashion. The positive responses you get will most likely request additional samples of your work, and that's when you follow up with your portfolio. If you live in an area where a lot of agents do business, there's nothing like the personal touch, especially if you have a talent for self-salesmanship and a little charm.

Advertising agencies don't usually work without agents but any enterprising, ambitious artist shouldn't take no for an answer; send off some material and see what happens. The art directors will always look at your portfolio, and they might be sufficiently impressed to file you away and give you a call when a new project presents itself—one they feel would be right for your style.

When it comes to contacting these agencies and art directors, sans agent you can employ the same basic mailing technique. First, gather the names of various art editors at the larger houses, submit your card and sit back and wait for a response. Lists of art directors can be purchased or you can use the cheaper avenue—your public library. There's a book known as the Red Book but actually entitled *Standard Directory of Advertisers;* be sure to use the most recent version (art directors do have a tendency to move about quite a bit) and compile your list for your mailing. After a decent interval has elapsed (give it a couple of weeks) you can make follow-up calls but be polite and don't be put off if you can't get through. Other than talent—courtesy, tenacity and patience are your most valuable assets.

If you have the financial wherewithal, you can advertise your wares (it is expensive) in *American Illustration Showcase, RSVP, Artist's Market* or others. It's how I chose and contacted many of the artists in this book. I thumbed through the pages, was struck by a particular artist's talent and contacted him or her.

Joining artists' organizations such as the American Institute of Graphic Arts or the Society of Illustrators can help to put you in contact with other illustrators, some of whom, like yourself, are trying to find their way into the business. You can attend seminars, learn from the pros and avail yourself of newsletters. It's a good idea, particularly if you consider yourself a social animal.

The markets are out there. It's a matter of finding the one where you feel your work honestly belongs and making a concerted effort to break down that set of doors. Trying to get into too many at once, especially at the beginning of your career, might spread you too thin and dissipate your energy. There are more markets out there for cartoonists and humorous illustrators than you might imagine. To get a head start, check out the appendices in the back of this book.

ILLUSTRATION

To illustrate really means to brighten, to light up, to elucidate. Illustration is one of those words that conjure up a variety of images to different people . . . and why? Because illustration as an art form has now become as varied as you can possibly imagine. It runs the gamut from the simplest cartoon sketch to the most complicated and detailed painting. Illustration is merely a graphic realization or extension of the text, so anything can qualify. On the other hand, a nice little cartoon sketch could metamorphose into an illustration merely by the application of other techniques, the definitive triumph of style over substance.

First of all, when you're approaching the basic concept of your illustration you should probably read and reread the material several times. Try to find that elusive hook upon which to hang your drawing (unless of course an art director has dictated the concept to you). But that's not usually the case since the things they're buying from you are your sense of humor and your conceptual abilities. Ask yourself which is the best way to communicate what it is you want to say visually. Perhaps an ink-and-wash is the best way to express this extension of the text, or you might want to do a scratch board, a painting or a pastel. Decide for yourself which of these really captures the feeling of the story or article, which embodies the essence, the real spirit of the piece, in the best visual terms.

A word of warning: If you're illustrating a dry treatise on the application of aluminum siding, you can't very well use a scantily clad couple lolling on a beach in some tropical clime. Well, I guess you could and you might even halt the browser in his or her tracks, but as they read on they would discover they'd been duped. You have to play fair. The illustration should be a visualization, an amplification of the theme of the story, or possibly that one critical moment upon which the piece hinges.

Kathie Abrams always loved to draw and doodle but she always drew the same things over and over again—"either flowers and happy faces or weird head and shoulders . . . sort of a manic-depressive doodler." She worked at art more seriously in college by studying art history but her heart was in the life drawing class. After college she went to New York City and landed a job at Doubleday as a reader of children's books. After two years of watching other people's illustrations coming through her office, alternately being intimidated and encouraged by the quality of the work, she decided to really pursue illustration as

a career. She enrolled in Parsons School of Design in New York City and after two years of study, she jumped into the illustration arena with both feet, making the rounds and doing all the things that young, eager artists are supposed to do.

She had her ups and downs, including having her portfolio of panel cartoons returned to her from *The New Yorker* magazine with a rejection slip, and to add insult to injury there were coffee stains on the portfolio and all over the first drawing. "There's a lesson to be learned here . . . never bring in originals . . . However," she adds, "they included a little 'Sorry about that' note and a ten-dollar bill." She was too naive at the time to know there were other magazines that might buy those cartoons but she soon learned.

Kathie finally got an assignment to do a children's book, which was followed by another and another, and soon the world of illustration opened up to her. Today she's an active and respected artist whose work graces many fields. Her

Daughters of Chutzpah

advice: "Beginning free-lancers should allow themselves some time to 'catch on'—maybe several years before all their income will come from free-lancing. There's no ceiling to what you can earn but there's no floor either."

Brian Ajhar is one of those rare artists who have a knack for taking the seemingly driest of topics and infusing them with interesting and amusing visual life. He began sketching when he was very young, preferring to draw grotesque characters, and the more eccentric the better. "I also read a lot of *The Brothers Grimm,* and learned to draw with brush-and-ink, everything from little elves to great giants, wicked witches and fairy princesses. They still show up in some of my drawings," says Ajhar. "Only this time you might see them cavorting on Wall Street or a corporate board room to illustrate articles in *Forbes, Business Week* or *Fortune.*" This illustration and the next three in this section reveal Ajhar's unique style.

After high school, Ajhar was a portrait painter for a short time but as he says, "I found humor the easiest way to communicate, so by combining illustration with my painting style and adding a bit of whimsy, an editorial art style evolved that has not only been profitable, but also artistically satisfying."

After graduating from Parsons School of Design, Ajhar made the usual rounds with a portfolio filled with a variety of techniques and approaches. The humorous ones attracted the most attention, so that's where he decided to concentrate his energies.

When Ajhar begins a project he does voluminous thumbnail sketches before deciding on the final idea. He then moves over to a tracing paper pad with his pencil until he finally completes the finished rough. Photocopies of these are then sent over to the client for approval. "A lot of the characters I do are in adverse situations. . . . I'd rather portray a character in trouble than a happy guy holding a tube of toothpaste, smiling because everything's going great."

Ajhar starts out with Koh-I-Noor Blackie pencil and works on illustration board. He then fills in the completed sketch with a combination of ink, watercolors and colored pencil, a technique which has evolved into his own unique style. "I hooked up with a rep about a year out of school, but it didn't work out. Then I was with one for five years and have had Pamela Korn repping me

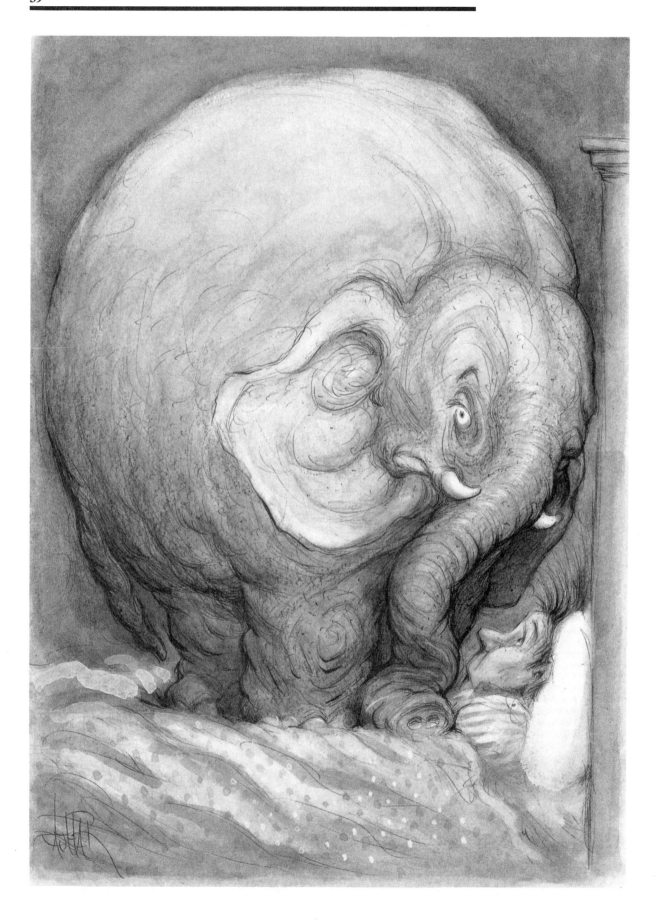

for the last two. It's working out real well." P.S. He also married her and they're very happy.

As far as advice to the new people coming into the business goes, Ajhar says, "I would tell him or her to work real hard at what you're good at and enjoy what you're doing. As far as the business side of it—just never quit, keep pushing, and if you believe strongly in what you are doing, somebody will use it, will find a way for it."

I illustrated an article a few years back regarding some actors' proclivities for deserting successful TV series to try for the brass ring of feature films and, in doing so, leaving the producers and cast members in the lurch. The material suggested that they had contracted "swelling of the ego," which caused them to seek greener (see money) pastures. By the by, it rarely worked. I chose to depict this ingrate's malady with the classic Jekyll-Hyde theme pictured here.

As you'll see in the next four drawings, Eldon C. Doty is an exceptionally skillful humorous artist. This might seem odd in light of the fact that he was a policeman for thirteen years. He always enjoyed drawing and cartooning but he never had the vaguest notion that he could make a living at it. However, when he retired at age thirty-eight, he decided to take some classes in fine arts. One of his instructors advised him that "if he wanted to make a living, "stay out of fine arts," so Doty obediently sold his house and moved to San Francisco to attend illustration school. He had intended to stay for a full three years but his portfolio so impressed one of his instructors that he was advised to quit after only a year and a half and go out into the commercial-art world and start selling his work. Again he wisely took a teacher's advice to heart.

Doty says, "I made up a portfolio of ten or fifteen pieces, mostly my student work, and started calling up art agencies and making appointments with art directors. I took the work, laminated them in plastic and put a nice felt backing on them. I believe your portfolio is important; it has to look nice. I learned a lot about portfolios in school and I was determined to have a portfolio that looked professional.

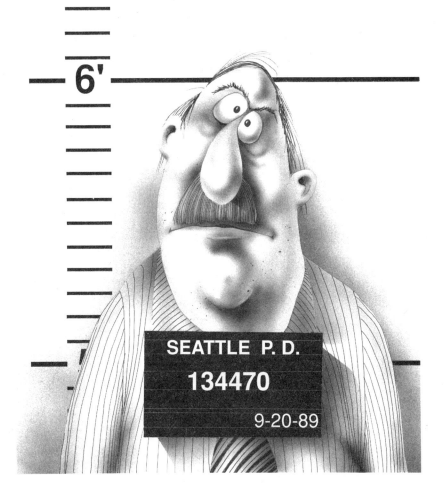

SEATTLE P. D.

134470

9-20-89

"I took my illustrations and actually put them in ads. I'd look through magazines and find an ad with a photograph or an illustration, then I'd cut out the original illustration and replace it with mine and then I'd photograph the whole thing. It looked professional. It was sort of a pasteup; it looked like I actually had done the work. The art directors never doubted that I had done the ad. They always seemed to prefer my humorous pieces so that's what I started doing more of. Police work breeds cynicism and that probably comes out in my art.

"I started getting assignments relatively soon and I've been active ever since. I went to New York for about a year and a half and then moved back to Seattle. Now I do all my business by fax (I just wonder how I ever got along without it) and Federal Express. Once you've established yourself as an illustrator you can live just about anywhere. Art directors used to be reluctant about hiring someone who didn't live in the immediate area but now they're getting used to it. I haven't seen a client in over a year."

Mary Grace Eubank doesn't consider herself a cartoonist, but whatever title you choose to assign to her she is nonetheless a wonderfully charming, humorous artist. Her contributions to "Sesame Street" are a mainstay of that organization, and her rounded, carefully airbrushed figures and characters, like the ones shown in the next two illustrations, are found in all the major markets. Her road to the world of illustration went from designing wrapping paper to greeting cards to working with "The Children's Television Workshop" and "Sesame Street." She feels that "if I had it to do all over again I think I would have gone to commercial art school. I think it's much more concentrated study, and you are exposed to more tricks of the trade. There's a lot of respect in the professional field for certain art schools."

But regarding illustration per se, she says, "Every time you do an illustration your ego is on the line. It's part of you; it's something you created. When it's rejected it's really difficult to keep in mind that it's not you, it's that piece of art that's being rejected. You develop confidence, but in the beginning it's very difficult. I had a hard time with that."

moon over my auntie

Michael Fleishman was a dedicated art education undergrad and now has an MA from Indiana University of Pennsylvania. He even taught fine arts for a while before he decided to toss his hat into the commercial-art ring to try to supplement his teaching income. He gave New York City a fling but Manhattan's breakneck pace and teeming masses weren't Michael's cup of tea, so he headed for Los Angeles, where his brother lives, to seek fortune (if not fame) as an illustrator. A "short stopover" to visit some friends in Kansas City turned into a full year; he liked the city immediately, plus it was, after all, where Hallmark Cards is headquartered. Perfect.

Michael admits to a few mistakes early in his commercial-art career. "I had this big monster of a portfolio and I had put just about everything in there I had ever done. It was this unwieldy whale." Fleishman was teaching full-time when he decided to approach Hallmark with his oversized but, needless to say, impressive portfolio. A secretary whisked it into the other room and he was told to return Wednesday. He did and found in the portfolio not only a rather

impersonal rejection note, but crumbs from someone's hasty lunch, and a few nail clippings. Luckily Michael had a solid sense of his talent so he was not discouraged by this apparently cavalier attitude toward his work.

He continued to pursue his goal, eventually visiting the *Kansas City Star* to show his work. He was finally hired (after having to await the outcome of the World Series) to do some cartoons on the editorial and business pages and his career was launched. After that he got more of his drawings published and he learned from studying his work in the paper that he had to simplify his style, "crosshatching and more delicate pen work didn't reproduce all that well so I had to go to work improving and cleaning up my technique." By this time, his portfolio was pared down to a more manageable size; he had tear sheets of many published pieces while the originals were safe at home. The unwieldy whale had become a sleek shark—lean and impressive. After more illustration work in various cities and a short stay as staff illustrator at Abbey Press, he finally found his way to Ohio, where he now lives, teaches and continues to successfully sell free-lance illustrations and cartoons.

Along the way he also became an author. His book *Getting Started as a Freelance Illustrator or Designer* is selling so well that he's been asked to do a second, and he's just accepted a position as contributing editor to *Artist's Magazine*.

© MICHAEL CARL FLEISHMAN

When Michael's not writing or teaching, he's in the studio. "Between the drawing, painting, self-promotion and marketing, you put in an eight-hour day. You have to sell yourself. It's a full-time job but you learn how really important marketing is. You get a rep only if they're better at selling your work than you are. An agent is going to be cut in for anywhere from 25 to 35 percent, so they better do the job for you. It's a numbers game, but are you spreading yourself too thin? Can you be a salesman and an artist? And how much energy do you have to do all this?"

I recently did a production of *They're Playing Our Song* and the producer wanted his own logo for the program (as opposed to the New York version). So, since the Neil Simon musical dealt with the up-and-down romantic involvement of a composer and a lyricist, I chose to picture the pair on a musical note, the girl perched on top and the man scaling the note in pursuit. Obvious? Maybe . . . So come up with a better one and draw it. There. I have cavalierly flung my gauntlet at you.

Gerry Gersten is a brilliant artist and caricaturist whose highly stylized work overlaps successfully into the illustrative area. His perceptive renderings are in constant demand by book clubs and literary societies. He has a "kind hand" for a caricaturist, meaning that he exaggerates without malice, which is a rare quality. His other work is no less impressive. His background in the public schools of the Bronx taught him little about art. At that time, he hated Norman Rockwell and loved Mondrian. Today (after having studied with Robert Gwathmey, a highly respected artist and teacher at Cooper Union in Manhattan) he has totally reversed those opinions. Gerry says, "A drawing is a picture of something or someone—a place, an incident, a mood. The artist or illustrator (the terms are interchangeable) draws from his own experiences and knowledge and describes, in a very unique and personal kind of writing, himself and the subject of his picture."

His caricatures, like this one of Ernest Hemingway, illustrate the Quality Paperback Book Club ads, as well as *Time, Newsweek, Esquire* and *GQ*. On the subject of caricature, he says, "I think you can learn from a caricature class certain ways to focus, to concentrate on things the masters have discovered. But you have to be a damn good drawer of anything to be a good caricaturist. Caricature can be taught, but the sensitivities cannot. It has to be part of your psyche—of who you are."

Chloraseptic

Gersten takes three to five hours to do the first rough of a caricature and he works almost exclusively with a pencil on a 14″ × 17″ sheet.

"There is an anxiety rather than a preference," says Gersten, "when it comes to caricaturing women. It is implied that you make women as pretty and attractive as can be. There is a certain caution artists have with women. You realize that men are fair game but you have to be nice to women."

Benton Mahan is an extremely versatile artist whose works range from children's books (you'll see some of that work in a later chapter) to mainstream advertising and spot drawings. Ben grew up on a farm in Ohio and his entire exposure to art was through magazines and books. He majored in illustration and while in college turned down a job with Hallmark to work for a small card company. From there he went on to New York and became a designer and soon was doing spot drawings. He finally returned to Hallmark, where he worked for a few years before striking out on his own as a successful free-lancer. He now also teaches illustration at his alma mater, the Columbus College of Art and Design.

"It's always a little difficult when you start out. I kind of phased into it, which I think is the best way to do it. I was living in an area where there was a lot of free-lance work available, so I didn't have too much of a problem keeping busy." He also adds, "I think it's important, when one has time, to keep drawing and painting, picking up new techniques and just learning from other people. Drawing is like playing the piano—it takes a lot of practice, and you have to practice continually."

Jeff Moores's visual world is a strange one; it's very rectangular and inhabited by small people. His style successfully combines whimsy, humor and charm. Even back as far as high school Jeff was an enterprising and talented guy. He started a T-shirt business that really helped to shape his unusual style of drawing little people. He helped to pay his way through the first college he attended with silk-screened T-shirts that pictured campus life and even included a few of his peers in the drawings. They were, needless to say, a hit. Jeff studied on what he calls "the five-year, five-school plan." He started out wanting to be a photographer and attended several schools until he decided, after taking a lot of rather dry chemistry classes, that photography was not for him.

He finally went to the Parsons School of Design in Manhattan and took a few more courses at Carnegie-Mellon before finally deciding to pursue art as a full-time occupation. His T-shirts went along as part of his portfolio and it was those "little people" that caught an art director's eye and gave him his first assignment. Jeff did illustrations, spots and cartoons for various magazines. He always had a fascination with photography, which led to an interest in film, which led ultimately to his sequential drawings. Those drawings got him into *New York* magazine and put his work on the map. His series of drawings entitled "Be Different" have been adopted by New York City as a total campaign.

One of the wildest artists I've come across in quite a while is the unique and very funny Steve Phillips. (You can judge for yourself by looking at the three illustrations in this section.) While still in high school, he was drawing satiric comic books based on his classmates. He took some design courses in college and in 1976, when the greeting-card companies were rather stale and nothing new or refreshing was available, he started designing his own cards and they took off. While working as a bartender part-time (a job he still loves because, according to him, "it's a great source of comedic inspiration"), he talked to a friend who suggested they go into business together licensing his drawings. He took his series on Melinda and her PMS attacks around until they were finally bought by Landmark Calendars, a very successful, rather avant-garde company (which is, incidentally, run almost entirely by women). Since then his licensing, which is a form of renting an image for other, ancillary markets such as T-shirts, mugs, cards, etc., is booming.

Steve adds, "The beauty of licensing is having just one drawing that can be marketed in several different ways." Insofar as selling the drawing, Steve says, "Almost every major city has a stationery gift show about five times a year, and all the major players, like the greeting-card industry, go there with all their products for store owners to buy. They also are open to looking for fresh talent. They don't promote doing that but you can show up with your portfolio, look around and see who's doing the kind of stuff that speaks your language . . . and talk to them. That's how we found Landmark Calendars."

At first Steve was concerned about women misunderstanding his intent. It was never to make fun of, but rather to laugh with women and their struggles. "We loved it because we could relate to it," says Patricia Sklar, president and owner of Landmark Calendars, a Novato, California, firm. "This company has mostly women executives, so we could really relate to PMS. . . . It's one of our top sellers every year."

Immediately after work, Melinda would "get away from it all" at her favorite little hide-a-way

Unable to revive her with a mere kiss, Prince Charming attempts to awaken a fatigued Sleeping Beauty with another approach

Steve adds, "The weird thing is that men go through these same mood swings, but they never admit it. I know there are times when I'd like to run off with the refrigerator."

But as far as work as a free-lancer is concerned, he states that "you still have to do the shopping whether you're successful or not. Even with an agent, you have to hustle all the time. Go to the stores and see who's doing work like yours and those are the people you should contact."

Spot drawings are just simple little humorous illustrations; they are basically decorative and serve to break up a page of rather dry text and aid the designer in his layout. However, the drawings are not arbitrary. Instead, they make a point by enhancing the text. They are sometimes more design than cartoon so the artist must have a special feel for this sort of work. I'd recommend thumbing through *The New Yorker,* or any tastefully realized magazine, to become aware of the spot drawings and their function. These drawings are not always humorous in nature; often they're merely eye-catching. On the other hand, you might even think of them as a panel cartoon minus a caption or real "gag."

Benton Mahan is a very prolific and sought-after spot artist. Here are a few samples of his work in that area.

It's wise to keep in mind that your spot drawing is going to be printed in an area approximately two inches square, so your drawing should be simple enough in concept and execution to reproduce well in that limited space. Keep it uncomplicated and clean; deal only with the essentials.

Books are an extremely fertile area for spot drawings. Whether it's the self-help line (you know the type: *How to Be in Love with Me*) or books on botany, barracudas, boxing, bell ringing (I feel an attack coming on) or bird watching (I'm better now). They're all in need of those little, seemingly insignificant drawings to break up the text.

Spot drawings don't necessarily come cheap, so if you do enough of them, small though they may be, at the end of the year you'll find that they've brought you a tidy little sum. One of the contributing factors to the lucrative aspect of this work is that you're paid another fee (usually about 10 percent of the original payment) each time they choose to use the drawing again. We're talking magazines, of course. Do enough of them and you can see how these might eventually mount up. It might not be a bad idea to include a page of spot drawings in your portfolio. It certainly does demonstrate style and versatility and willingness to accept this kind of assignment. For further information on spot drawings and other prices, consult the most recent edition of the Graphic Artists Guild handbook, *Pricing and Ethical Guidelines.* You can obtain it through the Graphic Artists Guild.

While we're at it, let's not ignore the humor book market. This is usually reserved for the better-known cartoon artists, but sometimes publishers will take a chance on someone new if the style is especially right for a certain piece of material that they've acquired. Again I suggest that you visit your bookstore and forage through the humor section. You'll see a broad range of cartoon styles and subject matter. Make a list of the most prolific humor publishers (including addresses) and begin sending them material. When it comes to books, the artist is usually paid a flat fee or you might get an advance payment against future royalties but pursue this humor area seriously (if such a thing can be done).

There are other, smaller markets that the illustrator can court. For instance, most small, independently owned businesses have in-house bulletins, memos, stationery and order forms and they need cartoons to brighten up these otherwise rather drab missives. They are a particularly good place for the newcomer to break in because they are always looking for new free-lance artists. There are many small companies out there so the law of averages is definitely working in your favor. Send samples of your work to travel agencies, small department stores, banks or any other local business that you think could use your services. Sometimes they have to be talked into it, cajoled a little.

When I was in the Navy I became aware of a fairly stringent food conservation drive that came directly from Washington in the form of a directive, so (never one to be shy) I approached the mess officer and offered to do a series of conservation cartoons all around the mess hall. He bought it; I did them and got out of a lot of nasty mess duty. The point being he wouldn't have thought of it if I'd not brought in some sketches and pitched the idea. So be resourceful, have a little initiative. A little controlled aggressiveness wouldn't hurt either.

There's also a rich market for the cartoonist's/illustrator's art in storyboards, best defined as a series of drawings usually used to aid the clients in picturing a proposed television commercial. They're not necessarily detailed drawings; they can be rather free renderings with the emphasis on the overriding concept. The art director will give you a set of sketches (usually from five to nine panels) from which you will produce the completed storyboard. It's not a difficult process but one that requires special knowledge.

There's another fairly new kid on the block in "animatics." It's another process with which you should acquaint yourself if you're really going to be a professional cartoonist/illustrator. Animatics are ostensibly drawings that are photographed with a moving camera, as opposed to static storyboards. Advertising agencies use them to create, for as little money as possible, the movement and overall feel of a TV commercial so that the clients can see it prior to the actual shooting. Quite often the ad idea will die before it takes off, the animatic having proven that it doesn't work. As with storyboards, there are specific guidelines and techniques required to work successfully in this area. Unfortunately, they'd require more room than I have in this chapter, so I highly recommend a fine book on these subjects, *Comps, Storyboards, and Animatics* by James Fogle and Mary E. Forsell. It's something well worth your time and further investigation.

As you can see, illustration runs the gamut: from the most formal, deliberate paintings to the wildest, most uncontrolled attacks upon paper with brush; from delicately airbrushed cartoons to splashy ink drawings; from gift papers and spot drawings to illustrating slick magazine stories. Never count yourself out as an illustrator, because there's room and opportunity for everyone and every approach. You merely have to find that happy marriage of content of subject and style that allows room for your personal vision and technique to flourish.

 PANEL CARTOONS

Panel cartoons have been a staple of American magazines since their inception. They used to be a regular feature of every major magazine in the U.S., but since the number of magazines has shrunk (unfortunately), so has the size of the panel (or gag) cartoon market. It's still a market to be courted, but to rely on it for financial sustenance is foolhardy. If you have some terrific gags, draw them up and send them off but don't hold your breath, and please don't depend on them for a source of revenue, just move on to the next project and hustle, hustle, hustle.

Most panel cartoons are a humorous reflection of the times in which we find ourselves, like them or not. If you want to feel the pulse of an era, look at its cartoons; they'll give you an encapsulated view of the world at that time. A lot of artists are producing rather fey, gentle, observational humor but I think it should be more funny than flimsy, satirical rather than sweet, biting rather than bland, comical rather than clever. (I know, I know, the alliteration thing again!) Here's an example from Borislav Stankovič.

As far as the draftsmanship of panel cartoons goes, I believe it's best to keep it simple unless you require an elaborate drawing to make a point. I saw a gag years ago that pictured an opulent, sumptuously decorated bedroom and a portly, mustachioed man kneeling at his bedside, his hands clasped in prayer. The caption read: "Please, sir, could I have more." The joke fuses a lot of elements—the satiric comment in his using the phrase from *Oliver Twist,* his greed and the fact that he actually believes that God, in his wisdom, would see fit to grant him "more." From our point of view, he has more than enough. But none of this humor would work if the drawing did not communicate to us his grandiose life-style.

In most cases, as in this example from Bob Vincke, simplicity works, so try not to clutter the panel with too much background or extraneous matter to distract the eye from its focus. The thrust of a clean, neat line is always visually arresting; your eye can follow simple lines easily and move directly on to the punch line. The viewer doesn't always possess the patience to linger over a drawing in order to ferret out the humor.

There *are* exceptions to that hard fast rule of simplicity (because of course there are no hard fast rules). However, I do recall a Charles Addams *New Yorker* cartoon picturing an audience reacting with shock and horror to some unseen film. In the center of this sea of horrified faces is one of the characters from his gallery of ghouls, and this one is smiling pleasantly, obviously enjoying

what the others are reacting negatively to. It took me a while to find that face but it was well worth the time and trouble. A similar gag was used with a mass of hysterical faces and in the back, subtly placed, difficult to spot at first, was the Mona Lisa smiling her inscrutable grin. The lesson to be learned here is that less is more. Don't confuse the issue; the picture should allow the viewer to instantaneously get the joke. Don't make them work at it.

Good competition is essential in panel cartoons. Composition is merely the art of directing the viewer's eye where you want it to go, making it see what you want it to see and in the order in which you choose. Here's a cartoon I came up with about two nuns. What's wrong with this picture?

I hope you spotted that the composition is lousy; your eye is wandering all over the place trying vainly to find a focus. There's another glaring error here and that is that the nun on the left is silent and the nun on the right is speaking. If you have two characters in a cartoon and only one is speaking (which is the norm), it's advisable to place the speaking character on the left, since we read from left to right. (For Hebrew magazines, of course, you'll have to make the necessary adjustment.)

Or if you choose to place two figures at either edge of the frame, there better be a good reason or a point to be made, i.e., to show the distance between them emotionally or psychologically à la the famous dining room scenes in *Citizen Kane;* as the couple grew further apart, so did the physical space between them. Otherwise, it's better to use a unifying background object between your characters—not to distract but to tie the figures together, to help lead the eye to the desired spot. In an office scene it could be a picture on the wall, a potted plant, a shadowy background figure—anything that serves to unite the elements in the frame.

In these examples, the nuns have been upstaged by the tree dividing them and the trees and buildings at the edges of the frame, which lead your eye away from the area of focus. If it weren't for the intense black of their habits, which acts as a magnet for the eye, you wouldn't care about them at all. In this next preliminary drawing I've amended a few problems but still the low horizon line leads your eye off the paper on either side. Still not good. An O, used as the basis for the figures and items in the frame, would lead the eye to the desired area and make the joke work better.

The trees and buildings should be only peripheral. Use them to establish mood and location but not to "upstage" the focus, that is, steal attention away from the central characters.

I think this next version has much better composition, you see the nuns quickly and easily and nothing else tugs at your eye for attention. In order to assess your composition objectively, when you finish a sketch hold it up in front of a mirror and see where your eye goes. Does it still travel to the desired area, the focus of the gag? And while you're there, notice how reading from right to left doesn't work.

I also chose to draw the nuns with a little more of a "casual" feel and to change their expressions slightly and do a background wash. A lot of cartoonists are fond of using wash on the background or less important aspects of the drawing; the wash helps to throw focus to the central characters.

I rewrote the gag line several times before I was satisfied. The first line was simple: "I see you have a new dress." I found that a little too bald, too pointedly "on the nose." I changed it to: "Oh, Sister Margaret, I see you have a new dress.'' I could hear the reading I wanted in my head but the words didn't do it for me. I wanted more of an ''attitude'' from the nun who was speaking. I thought it deepened the humor a bit. I finally ended up with a line that made the nun a bit judgmental and maybe a tad catty but the joke remains—how can you tell if a nun has a new dress? You can't. So the final version of the line is ''Well, Sister Margaret, another new dress?'' I think it's terse enough, and it becomes more character humor regarding nuns and their attitudes, maybe it helps to humanize them. Some people still think of nuns as pious penguins. But more about gags a little later on.

In the world of the panel cartoons there aren't many subtleties or nuances; you pretty much have to deal in broad-stroked stereotypes. Bankers all wear three-piece suits, are middle-aged and portly; the reality of a young, slim banker doesn't work unless you're making a point or you can sell his profession in another way.

In your cartoons, you should communicate instantly who these people are, where they are, what they do, what they're doing or where they're going. Firemen always wear helmets, gangsters wear black shirts and white ties, prisoners wear numbers emblazoned on their chests. Props are critical. Lawyers and business-men all tote briefcases and secretaries carry steno pads.

The arena or setting in which the characters appear can be merely a suggestion or a complex drawing, depending upon its importance to the gag. And here clichés abound also. Hollywood is palm trees and sunglasses, and New York is tall buildings. In this cartoon by Charlie Rodrigues, it doesn't take much to show you that they're inside an airplane.

But how do these guys create jokes? And how do we come up with a single panel drawing that evokes a laugh or at least a smile? Well, it starts with a jaundiced view of the universe and its inhabitants (which you probably have or you wouldn't have picked up this book in the first place). It's staying alert . . . it's walking into a restaurant and when asked if you want smoking or nonsmoking, carrying that to the next ridiculous extreme . . . fuming? On fire? Possibly picturing three sections, one with a man impatiently waiting for his late date (or meal) and doing just that—FUMING.

In order to get into this field, start looking around you and shift your mind into that satirical gear. Have fun with the things you observe every day, carry the simplest occurrence or trend to a ridiculous extreme and you'll find humor waiting around the corner. Make a list of the irritating things you encounter every day and you'll have found a lot of fuel for your cartoons. It's OD'ing on a song. I heard "Tomorrow" (as in the sun will come out tomorrow) from *Annie* three times in one day on a radio station and immediately pictured two guys crossing the desert baked by the scorching sun. One of them is singing at the top of his lungs, the other is doing a "hate take." Takes are important. You have to be able to draw a character in many moods, active as well as reactive. Charlie Brown has a wonderful crooked-mouth grim look that he does right out to us that speaks volumes.

♪ THE SUN WILL COME OUT TOMORROW—BET YOUR BOTTOM DOLLAR THAT TOMORROW... ♪

How did my mind lead me to that joke? I tried to re-examine the process and I concluded that the song and the word "sun" being repeated over and over again got to me and that led me to thinking how it would be if you were where there was nothing but sun and I went right to the old generic two-guys-lost-in-the-desert gag. It provided me with a fresh twist on a very old situation.

Look around you and become an astute observer of the world. Wherever you are, someone is doing or saying something silly, stupid, outrageous, pithy or pathetic (we're all funny in our own way) intentionally or otherwise. Watch the interview shows on television for one afternoon and jot down all the really inane things said by guests and hosts alike. There's a lot of material there.

There are only a few basic types of panel cartoons but several roads to use to get to them. There's the *silent* cartoon, in which the picture speaks for itself, no words are necessary—not only are they superfluous but they'd probably hurt the joke. These cartoons are welcomed by editors because they cross over language barriers and have potential for reprinting in other markets. Try to honestly assess your gag and determine whether it requires words or whether it is better and funnier without them. Here's an example from Joe Szabo.

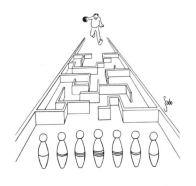

Then there's the totally *verbal* cartoon, which uses a drawing only to establish location and characters. A drawing of two men carrying briefcases on a city street reveals their approximate ages, that they're businessmen and that they live in the city. They could be saying anything to each other, the words are not tied in with or dependent upon the drawing. Here's an example of a purely verbal gag. Take away the drawing and the line still works.

In the *combination,* it's necessary to see something in order to get the joke. As with the nuns gag, you have to see the nuns and be reminded of the undistinguished nature of their garb. How does she know the other one has a new dress? It's silly but that's the humor. Here's a good example of this by Moore.

"Hello, sir, I'm a free-lance pepper grinder, only one dollar."

The *contrast* gag works in the same way. You have to see the arena or the way a character is dressed or a particular item—something that helps you to understand the gag.

Here's another example of a contrast gag. The scene is a run-down shack filled with old newspapers, and plates piled in the sink; a man in an undershirt sits at a rickety kitchen table, a woman in a robe and curlers is on the wall phone and barking to her husband, "It's a PBS poll. What'd you think of Oscar Wilde's *The Importance of Being Earnest* as executed by the BBC repertory?" Would that be funny in a palace? Of course not. It's the contrast that makes it work.

Then there's the *litotes* gag (one of my favorite offbeat words meaning "extreme understatement"), like walking into a palatial residence and telling the hostess, "Nice little place you've got here." A wonderful example of a litotes was James Thurber's classic cartoon depicting a swordsman decapitating his opponent with one swift stroke. The caption read "Touché." No additional words or embellishments could possibly be funnier.

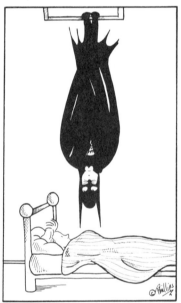

His sleeping habits were definitely putting a strain on their relationship

Steve Phillips, in his wonderfully bizarre world, is as good a purveyor of litotes gags as anyone. His series on Melinda has been used for calendars, datebooks, greeting cards—you name it, he's done it. Here's a prime example of that kind of approach to humor, that is to say a wild, exaggerated drawing or situation where the verbiage is understated to the point of being ludicrous.

Then there's *superior position,* which usually involves a hidden element, something the viewer sees or is aware of that the character is not. It's a staple of comedy films in that we, the audience, are shown something of which the protagonist is unaware, like the classic banana-peel gag. We know it's there so we are allowed to anticipate the outcome and view the unsuspecting victim with "superior position"—we know what they don't know and in our warped way

Melinda prepares a little demonstration to help
Barney fully understand the kind of day
she was having

we can't help but find this funny. This is also used extensively in horror or suspense films. We know that the woman shouldn't go into the fruit cellar because Norman Bates's mother is waiting down there with a knife, so we react accordingly. Steve Phillips also used that device for this cartoon.

Then there's *character* comedy, which is based on prior knowledge of a character or a group of characters. We know them so well that they don't have to do much to make us laugh . . . like the Charles Addams gallery or Gahan Wilson. We know where these people are coming from, their attitudes are clear, the joke is easy for us to understand because it stems from an already familiar point of view. Knowing Archie Bunker's social biases, all you had to do was to have him answer the door and find one of several ethnic groups standing there; we filled in the humor because we almost knew what his reaction would be before he did.

Another classic Charles Addams cartoon takes place on a narrow, winding mountain pass road; an impatient driver is stuck behind Uncle Fester, who waves at him to go around. From our vantage point we can see a huge truck barreling around the curve toward them. The outcome is obvious but then of course we're already tuned in to the character of Fester, which helps us to get the joke quickly. This is comedy based on character *and* superior position. We know Fester's proclivity for pain and evil, *and* we see the truck coming, which the unsuspecting driver does not. Interestingly enough, if this joke were carried one step further, the humor would disappear completely. For instance, if we saw the driver's face it might change our attitude; put a pretty young woman or children or a dog in the car and you would no longer be amused. Plus you're not really seeing the car go over the cliff; the humor stems from the fact that Uncle Fester *wants* him to go around. If he actually does it, the joke turns tragic and the humor is gone.

It's true that whenever we become familiar with the traits, flaws, weaknesses or neuroses of characters and we can predict their response in any given situation, we laugh in anticipation of their reaction. Garfield is a good example of this. We expect him to be outrageous and outspoken and so we enjoy his antics. Of course Garfield has another edge, he's a cat. You can get away with a lot by using animals as your central characters. Gary Larson of The Far Side has tapped into that humor vein and been enormously successful with it . . . and deservedly so.

And last, but certainly not least, is the *generic* cartoon, a scene or situation that we've seen so many times that it's like meeting an old friend. The two men in the desert (as in the "Tomorrow" gag we saw earlier) and the man and woman on the desert island are situations that have what seem to be a mine of endless variations. A really good and challenging exercise is to try to come up with something fresh and new for these time-honored situations. It's not easy but it's fun.

Okay, so now it's time to create some gags. Cartoonists and gag writers use several approaches. Some sit and think and make notes. Others doodle until a face or a scene or something inspires them to be funny, while others plod away relentlessly with a scene or situation in front of them. They keep going until something strikes them. I like to look through magazines like *Life, People* or *National Geographic,* anything that has pictures. I find it inspires me to come up with gags. Look at a scene and try to find that twist, that unexpected turn that surprises and amuses. Or carry a situation one step further, and then further, and then to its ultimate extreme.

This artist, Turhan Selcuk, took a simple image, that of a group of people using binoculars, and went just one step further with it to make it a little insane. Also, I don't think it would've been as funny if they had been pointing away from us or to the side. It's not only better composition but it's more of a direct threat to us, the viewers.

Unless you're a doodler who gets inspiration from that kind of activity, don't even sit down to your drawing board until you have a gag, a vague idea or just a whimsical thought in mind. Think about what has occurred during the day of a funny, or even potentially funny, nature. Did you overhear an exchange between a couple that was deadly serious but you wanted to supply the punch line? Can you recreate that moment? Usually when we're emotionally involved in a situation we aren't always able to see the humor, but later on, we dearly hope, we can sit at a safe distance in a comfortably objective seat and finally see the ridiculousness of our behavior. As someone once said, "Comedy is tragedy plus time." We have that advantage as gag writers; we can be the objective eye that sees the humor around us clearly and instantaneously. So keep alert and look around you, especially in your own life and household. Steve Phillips, the cartoonist who began as a bartender, knows the value of that job. He encounters more humanity letting its hair down and more funny material in one night than you could ever use. The human comedy is going on around us all the time—just tap into it, watch it unfold and use it.

Okay, so let's say that you have two dozen hysterically funny, beautifully drawn cartoons. Now what? Just for the fun of it, take a ride or walk over to your local magazine stand—I mean one of those that really specialize in all kinds of magazines—and see what's out there. It's pretty amazing . . . *Monthly Manicurist, Guns Galore, Chiropractic Confessions* . . . The list goes on and on. And a lot of them buy cartoons. True, they have to fit into their particular format but they do buy panel cartoons. And it's probably easier to get your feet wet on a smaller level with smaller magazines. The competition isn't as keen and, of course, the money isn't as good, but when you're trying to build a career, to get a foot in the door, it doesn't matter. Just get into print.

Examine the magazines carefully and assess their editorial policies; obviously you're not going to be sending racy cartoons with skimpily clad girls to *Religion Today,* but try to get a feel for what the cartoon editor is looking for and see what you have (or you can create) that's right up his humor alley.

Roughs are fine if the editor knows your work or has seen completed cartoons by you in the past; but if you're an unknown quantity to them it's best to include at least one completed drawing so that you can show your real finish technique. But once you're established, roughs will do just fine.

It's perfectly acceptable to submit cartoons on bond typewriter paper, size 8½″ × 11″. The only danger is that they'll curl up from wash, so if you're a wash artist use a heavier stock. I'd recommend sending about ten at a time; don't overwhelm them, but don't let them think you're short on inspiration, either— so (and this is a very subjective decision) I think ten is about right.

Incidentally, when you send in finished art it can be patched or quilted, as long as it reproduces well it doesn't matter. Quilting is when you've taken a second look at a drawing and decided that you like the drawing but you'd like to change the face or the expression on the central character. You can fix the problem easily; it's one of the uses of rubber cement that I mentioned in the section on materials. Make a machine copy of the old face, place it on your light box and draw the preferred version on top of it. Then cut that out carefully and rubber-cement it in place right over the old face. You'd be amazed at the amount of artwork that comes in with multiple patches affixed to it—hence the term quilting. Of course, when it's shot for publication all of that disappears and only the clean drawing emerges. It's a great time-saving device and it allows you the luxury of retaining the parts of the drawing that you're particularly pleased with. You can use this technique to replace clothing, signs, shoes, any item or portion of the drawing that you wish. Some people prefer to spray the back of the patch with Spray Mount (available at all art stores) and then put it into place; but experiment, a little trial and error (actually a lot of error at first) and soon you'll be proficient in this wonderful labor-saving technique. Other artists prefer piecing the drawing together and using tracing paper or their light board to make a new clean copy, but again, try both and use the one that works best for you.

Multiple submissions are not a particularly good idea. You could get yourself into a bind by having to explain to one magazine that another magazine just purchased that cartoon and before you know it you've made an enemy unnecessarily.

Don't let an editor rewrite your gag line or redo your drawing unless he consults you first. He might be brilliantly gifted and helpful and be of enormous benefit, but then there's always the other possibility. He could screw up a good thing, so—novice or not—stick to your guns and insist that you have the last creative word.

You can obtain lists of the art editors at the various magazines by looking through either the *Writer's Digest* or the *Writer's Yearbook*. They have up-to-date listings on all the publications that are buying cartoons. With the current attrition rate of magazines, if I were to put a list in here, by the time this book goes to press it would be obsolete. Check out the library; it'll have just what you need. So come on, get busy . . . get drawing . . . get funny.

COMIC STRIPS

The art of the comic strip is an extremely diversified one; compare, if you will, the almost childish but effective drawings of Drabble as opposed to the more intricate style of something like Pogo or Apartment 3G. Comic strips to me are like writing and directing your own mini-movies. Some prefer a static camera technique that allows the characters to move around in the frame, while others use angles, close-ups, dramatic lighting, over-the-shoulder shots and generally more sophisticated approaches.

If you elect to draw a more realistic strip you'll need all those techniques and interesting angles in order to maintain viewer interest. The plot lines move slowly à la soap operas, but let's face it, they are soap operas. Strips like the aforementioned Drabble, and Peanuts and Andy Capp use primarily a locked-off-camera technique where the angle rarely changes. They might pop in now and then for a medium shot or a close-up but usually they stay well back and observe the characters' interaction, much like silent films and the movies of the early thirties did. Other strips, like Calvin and Hobbes and Doonesbury, utilize more variety in their format. G. B. Trudeau's Doonesbury has undergone an interesting visual metamorphosis in the past several years; the longer the strip continued, the more sophisticated the art became. The rather simple line drawings were replaced with better artwork as shading and interesting angles crept into the strip—and a better artist slowly emerged.

It took Calvin and Hobbes only three years (very short in comic-strip time) to achieve the incredible popularity it's now enjoying. This charming strip, which chronicles the adventures of a small boy and his imaginary pet tiger, depicts everything from the child's point of view. It is now published in more than 500 newspapers, which is especially rare since Watterson firmly has refused any merchandising offers, lucrative though they may be.

Calvin and Hobbes © 1989 Bill Watterson. Reprinted with permission of UNIVERSAL PRESS SYNDICATE. All rights reserved.

Watterson draws his strip with a distinctive yet uncluttered style that has great visual appeal. He has a knack for establishing a scene with a minimum of props or background; often it's a combination of words and picture that tells you where you are. Also, in the last panel, note how easily he accomplishes a change of scene.

Comic strips are a full-time job. To turn out a daily strip and a Sunday version is no mean trick, so when you submit to the various syndicators be sure your characters are rich enough to supply you with plenty of stories. And I wouldn't suggest hitting them with more than one strip concept at a time since it only muddies the waters. If they turn you down (and most likely the first time around you'll get plenty of rejections) then switch to Plan B and send in your next strip idea. And *never* send originals, always send photocopies. It's better to draw the originals with permanent ink; it's blacker and registers better for reproduction. You can use the nonphoto blue pencil for the finished drawings but do your preliminary sketches with a good #2 pencil. I'd advise against using a felt-tip pen for your work. The black is not deep or strong enough for good reproduction. A brush with India ink will always do the job for you so if your strip needs the loose, uncontrolled feel that a brush provides, that's the way you should go.

Fox Trot by Bill Amend is a fairly new arrival on the comic scene but it's currently holding its own. It's an odd mélange of strange-looking (and stranger-behaving) teenagers, and the strip is more verbal than most but it works. He has a great ear for teenage dialogue so there's a wonderful ring of truth about the way the characters speak and interact. You'll notice that his backgrounds are virtually nonexistent; they aren't needed because of the way he structures his stories.

Fox Trot © 1991 Bill Amend. Reprinted with permission of UNIVERSAL PRESS SYNDICATE. All rights reserved.

In the beginning you can make your panels any size and shape that you wish, within the normal format, but ultimately you'll have to conform to the dimensions prescribed by the editor or the syndicate. Later on you'll find it's wise to conform to a constant outer shape that allows the editor the freedom to place your strip into any format he chooses, thus untying his hands creatively and perhaps guaranteeing you a slot on the Sunday page. There are ½-page formats, ⅓-page formats and tabloid but each syndicate has its own mechanics and it's too early for you to worry about that. Sell the strip *then* worry. So keep it simple in the beginning; later on when you're a giant success you can make all sorts of demands.

Lettering is an extremely important aspect of strips, so important in fact that it's probably wisest to draw the balloons and the text first and then fit your characters into the remaining space. For instance:

The lettering should be legible; don't get sloppy or too fancy here, you can do it with your art but not the text. There are really only a few lettering styles so you should familiarize yourself with them and practice until it becomes as effortless as your drawing. Sketch out the three basic shapes of lettering, *circle, square* and *triangle*, and practice lettering until you become adept. It's a useful tool that will always come in handy if you're to continue in this crazy, capricious, cuckoo, charismatic career . . . cartooning. (I did it again—my apologies!)

If you don't have a great gift for lettering you can always use plastic lettering guides, available at all art stores. They help to neaten up your work, but they rob it of any style so it's still better to learn to letter.

PAMELA

A I3 C D E F G H I J K   L M N O   P R S T U

YOU CAN BE LOOSE..../
BUT NOT SLOPPY!
MAKE AN 'A' LIKE THIS A
NOT LIKE THIS A

I like to use a calligraphy pen with permanent ink. It has a wide point that becomes thinner when it turns naturally in your hand. This makes it an effective lettering tool.

You can be creative within the confines of those letters by making them bold or using italics to stress a point, and there's always exclamation marks and other punctuation. Also, don't crowd your balloons; make sure there is a comfortable margin around the text so that it's easy to read.

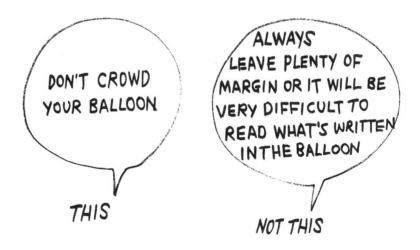

DON'T CROWD YOUR BALLOON

THIS

ALWAYS LEAVE PLENTY OF MARGIN OR IT WILL BE VERY DIFFICULT TO READ WHAT'S WRITTEN IN THE BALLOON

NOT THIS

Sketch your lettering in first, then the balloons and then the figures or scenes. Balloons come in a variety of shapes and sizes—all designed to accomplish different things. Here are some examples. This usually means the character is thinking:

An idea (of course). No one's found anything better:

Sadness or melancholy:

Anger or loud speech can be shown this way:

Walt Kelly (of Pogo fame) went even further. He had a character called the Deacon speak in Gothic type to differentiate his way of speaking. A gimmick like that has to be used sparingly.

Brian Basset draws his clever strip Adam with elegant understatement, a tasteful use of solid blacks and a wry sense of humor. It's extremely easy to read and understand and yet he's able to utilize various lettering styles to their maximum effect. You can't separate the lettering from the strip; the style is every bit as important as the drawing of the characters. It's a package deal, so don't weaken one aspect of it by not learning to letter. This strip is an excellent example of how it should be done.

Silhouettes are very effective in comic strips, even in humorous ones, because the solid black grabs your attention. However, they shouldn't be used when the characters are static. The characters should be involved in running or jumping or reacting—any really demonstrative physical action.

Now let's talk about the layout or composition of the strip. It should be sketched out only after you've come up with the story. It is a story even if it's told in only four or five panels, so tell yourself the tale and then decide how best to illustrate it. The "point of attack" is crucial. Do you discover these people in the midst of an argument? Are they outside? Inside? Who dominates the frame? Do you want to wait until the third frame to reveal the second character? Does it help the gag that we don't know who is being addressed?

Here's a sample strip I created for purposes of illustration. The first panel establishes the place, the mood and the character. The second elaborates on the theme to make sure that the reader understands the cliché and the reference (and to playfully tell them where you're heading). The third is the "switch," and the fourth the explanation (or punch line in this case).

It doesn't take much to establish a scene; use as little props and scenery as you possibly can. For instance, here's a scene with a young boy. All we have to see is a banister and it tells us that we're inside a two-story home. Often the merest suggestion is more effective than a complete interior rendering.

Here's another example: a strip I designed with Norman Liebmann that we called The Survivors (since it's about a rat and a roach). The first panel has to tell us where we are—this is the "establishing shot"—and the characters we are dealing with, the Rat and the Roach. I did something a trifle unconventional here in that at the edges of the panels I tried to give the effect of pipes running throughout the entire strip.

In comic strips excess verbiage is a definite no-no. You have to learn to be concise, terse, simple. You should pare down your language, use economy of words, rephrase and paraphrase until you make your point in as few words as necessary to make the gag work. The less to read the quicker the viewer gets to the joke or the point. I don't have to reiterate all that about the limited attention span of most Americans, do I? So keep it simple, uncomplicated, clean and to the point. When you finish a rough of the strip, use the old mirror trick— look at its reflection for an objective view, see if it works. Is it cluttered or hard to see? If so, rework it and simplify, simplify, simplify.

There are several different inking techniques that make comic strips more visually appealing. I think that textures are an enriching agent. Here's a figure drawn in several stages with different textures applied for interest. They not only lend it visual interest, but I believe the textures are helpful in establishing character. For instance, a tweed coat tells you something about the character who wears it. Look at your favorite strip closely and see how many different textures and techniques are used.

On the last one I cheated. I used what is called a mechanical tone (sometimes still known as Ben-Day). These sheets come in an incredibly wide range of designs and patterns. (Your local art store might even have the catalogue on

video now.) They're extremely easy to use and most effective. Some artists merely indicate where they want these used and it's done by the publisher.

There's another product that I find a little easier to use because you don't have to cut and peel. That's Instantex by Letraset, and it has transfer patterns in a fairly wide variety that you can "burnish" on. It's a little more controllable and doesn't require such fine cutting techniques (I'm a little sloppy when it comes to this stuff). This fellow's hair and pants were done with Instantex.

As were the second guy's hair and sweater.

Cathy Guisewite's cathy® has been a stunning success in the comic-strip world. This artist tapped into a rich vein of humor to which America (and especially young women) has responded. Her drawings are simple but effective; her change of scene in the last panel is accomplished neatly and she uses mechanical tones sparingly but very well. In the second panel she even uses one to gray the background and help the central figures stand out nicely.

cathy® © 1989 Cathy Guisewite. Reprinted with permission of UNIVERSAL PRESS SYNDICATE. All rights reserved.

There are actually only a couple of categories of strips: there's the self-contained joke strip like B.C., Momma, Garfield, and Calvin and Hobbes, and there's the serialized strip like Brenda Starr, Little Orphan Annie and Apartment 3G. (Naturally we're not discussing the single-panel series like Gary Larson's The Far Side or Charlie Rodrigues's Charlie, since we covered that genre in the chapter on panel cartoons.)

Insofar as ideas for strips go, you should always try to come up with a concept that has never been done, but it also has to contain that universal appeal. It should touch something in everyone. The success of Calvin and Hobbes is that almost everybody invented an imaginary creature or friend when they were a child, or knew a child who did. The Charlie Brown gang from Peanuts are all symbols of the adults that people our society, and Charlie Brown is the quintessential, put-upon everyman. So, in designing a strip try to find that common human denominator that reaches out to people. Even B.C., The Wizard of Id and other seemingly outrageous premises laid outside the norm have the human heart at their base; we identify with the characters' needs, greed, selfishness or other human foibles, and therein lies the basis for the humor. These are the qualities that editors look for in a new strip: audience identification, arresting visual style, consistency and, of course, humor. And it doesn't need to be fall-down funny. How many times have you actually laughed out loud when reading a strip? It can be gentle human humor or merely whimsical. Don't go for the big laugh since chances are you won't get it.

Your central characters, your protagonists, have to have appeal, they can't be totally negative. They can be flawed, like Andy Capp, but we forgive his flirting and pub-crawling because he's endearing in every other way. However, he's on the edge. If you were to take him a couple of steps further and have him actually consummate his flirtations or abuse his wife, then the strip would not only *not* succeed but it probably would never have been published in the first place. As an example, the strip that I showed you earlier, The Survivors, was one that I submitted to various syndicates several years ago. The rejection message was always the same: They felt that a rat and a roach were negative images and therefore not appealing enough to be lead characters in a strip.

Another quality that your lead character must have is interesting traits and personality quirks. We dealt with this in the Panel Cartoon section, but we, the audience, must know this character sufficiently that we think we can predict his or her response to a given situation. We take comfort in predicting their reactions because it gives us (here it comes again) superior position.

To get ideas for strips, look through the Sunday comics section and try to find what they're lacking. What kind of strip could you provide that they don't have? Trying to compete with Peanuts or B.C. would be silly—better to fill a void. All the draftsmanship for strips doesn't have to be highly skillful. The premise, emotional content and attitude of some strips lend themselves to a more casual, undefined art that some might call sloppy or undisciplined. That may be, but if it works for that particular strip there's no argument. Study the strips, their rhythms, the way they express themselves. It's important to have each character speak in a way that differs from the others; it helps to make a much-needed separation between them, and it clarifies things for the reader.

Their way of speaking should be almost as unique to them as their physical appearance, which should be clearly defined. We have to know who we're looking at instantly. It's one of the reasons that many cartoon characters always wear the same clothes. A grungy thought, it's true, but it's a simple identification device that works.

The first thing to do is get the idea for the strip, then design the characters and the situation, then come up with the gag, then the dialogue, then plot out the panels with the balloons and *then* finish the drawing. It's the last step in the process. Too many people I know sit down and try to start drawing a strip. I don't think that works because you get too involved in the drawing process and subliminally one thinks that the art can make anything happen when actually the reverse is true. The idea and the gag have to be strong; first the script *then* the actors.

When you get a rough sketch done, before doing the finished drawing, switch over to a heavy tracing pad; it's a great time-saving device. You can correct any mistakes as you go, and if you aren't pleased with the final result you can do it again from the second version. Once satisfied, just bring out the opaque white, clean up the messy areas and get it ready to send off.

The syndicates want to see about twelve completed strips from a newcomer and then about twelve more roughs, so you'd better create some characters that are rich enough to lend themselves to plenty of gags and stories. Research the Sunday funnies regarding sizes and dimensions and work no more than twice as big, otherwise it will get unwieldy. You can always have the work reduced back down on a good copying machine before you send it off. And always make a copy of everything for your files. If you wish, you can include a brief letter of self-introduction in which you discuss the strip and say where you see it going in the years (don't you wish) to come. I think the personal touch is always appreciated by art editors and buyers.

Some of the syndicates you can contact include Tribune Media Services, the Cartoonists & Writers Syndicate, Universal Press Syndicate and King Features. I list a few more in Appendix B, but I suggest consulting either *The Writer's Yellow Pages* or the most recent version of *Editor & Publisher Syndicate Directory* for a complete listing. There are hundreds of syndicates but only about ten major ones, so those are the ones to pursue. After all, you might as well shoot for the moon. Same postage.

Very few strips succeed in the way that Peanuts, for instance, has. That's the elusive brass ring to which every comic-strip artist aspires, but short of that there's still a good living to be made even with a modestly successful strip. And remember, it's primarily the merchandising that brings in the major part of the revenue, not the strip. But you have to get hot before they want to market your characters, so get busy, come up with a brilliant idea, work on it, perfect it and send it off. Remember, all cartoonists were once where you are right now. If it could happen to them, it can happen to you.

POLITICAL CARTOONS

Part caricature, part commentary, part editorial, political cartoons are a force in American politics, and woe be the politician or public figure who's targeted and attacked by a prominent, respected (and worst of all . . . funny) political cartoonist. They can bring a laughably negative spotlight to shine in your direction and that is extremely hard to live down much less erase forever. Says Paul Conrad of the *Los Angeles Times,* "Cartoons are ridicule and satire by definition."

When an artist decides to throw his or her hat into the area of political, or editorial cartooning (whichever you prefer), right away he or she has automatically alienated half of the population. Like a president taking the oath, you know going in that half of the people hate you or at least don't agree with you. But political cartoonists are a hardy breed for they churn them out daily, no easy task, like the proverbial salmon heading upstream. Now, that said, how many of you still want to try your hand at editorial cartooning? How many? Good. You're the ones I want to talk to.

First, you have to understand that this is a difficult and highly specialized area of cartooning. Most papers prefer buying from syndicates; it's cheaper and the product is established, hence more reliable. But that doesn't mean that out of the thousands of newspapers in this country you won't be able to crack through. It does, however, require more than passion, persistence and determination. You have to have that semi-caustic, satirical sense of humor that makes the editorial cartoonist cook. Jeff MacNelly, one of the most highly

respected of his breed, claims that he knows "many cartoonists who, if they couldn't draw, would be hired assassins." However, MacNelly has also said he believes that "you can get the reader's attention and hold it better through humor than with a hatchet."

Unfortunately, in this area of cartooning there's no formula, no recipe for breaking down those newspaper doors. Entree to those offices is difficult, but if you truly believe in your abilities and feel that you were meant to be an editorial cartoonist and nothing can dissuade you, then continue after it until you plain wear them down. I wish there were another way.

One thing you'll notice I'm sure is that most editorial cartoons are dependent upon caricature. If you have that ability it's a plus but I don't think it's absolutely necessary. There are ways around it, by using tags, labels, nameplates, etc., but if you have that gift for capturing the essence of someone in a few swift strokes, you're ahead of the game. If you don't, I'd recommend you get busy with some books on caricature (I even wrote one myself a few years ago) and start on it immediately. Of course, some faces are harder to do than others. Initially President Bush was hard to do, having what you'd call a rather nondescript face, but once his caricature was established others took it and ran with it. Much like a vocal impression, no one did Jack Nicholson until one guy came up with the key, and eventually everyone could imitate the imitator.

Political cartoons have to be current, topical, hot and fresh. There's nothing unfunnier than an old political cartoon whose allusions or personalities have been dimmed by the passage of time. You must be politically astute and well informed and have a working knowledge of history.

And yet it's amazing how little is required to get a point across. When the Jim Jones-Guyana-poisoned-Kool-aid tragedy occurred, I thought of a simple (yet I felt eloquent) drawing that said it all—a rendering of the famous (at the time) smiling Kool-aid pitcher, but now the mouth was simply turned downward in a melancholy expression.

In political cartoons, if you're admiring the artwork while the message slips by, then the cartoonist hasn't done his job. The mastery of Paul Conrad is his innate sense of how best to present his daily statement, and although he's an

extremely talented graphic artist he doesn't always utilize those abilities. He chooses not to in order to better make his point. Some sage pointed out that a good cartoon is 75 percent idea and 25 percent drawing. In the political cartooning arena this is certainly true. Rollin Kirby, an early cartoonist, once remarked that "a good idea has carried many an indifferent drawing to glory, but never has a good drawing rescued a bad idea from oblivion." So again it starts with the concept, the word. Lasting art is that rare perfect amalgam of art and idea—each one lending succor to the other. "Ideas are the toughest part—ideas that suit you and your manner of expression," says Pat Oliphant, the highly successful cartoonist.

Effective political cartoons have helped shape the destinies of public figures more than once. We all know how Thomas Nast exposed Boss Tweed in that famous event, but how many other times has a cartoon had some subtly insidious effect on the public when holding someone up to ridicule? These cartoonists are a rare breed—artists who are not timid about expressing their personal point of view and can do it humorously day after day.

©1991 Jimmy Margulies, *The Record* (NJ). Reprinted by permission.

Jimmy Margulies is the editorial cartoonist for *The Record* in the New Jersey suburbs. He attended Carnegie-Mellon University and began drawing cartoons and publishing them in the campus newspaper. He became a free-lancer for a while and then joined the *Army Times* as a regular contributor and was printed in *The Journals*, where he won several awards. He worked at *The Houston Post* for six years, which led to his assignment for *The Record*. He's won too many awards to mention and does work for, or has been reprinted in, *Time, Newsweek, Business Week,* and *U.S. News & World Report.* He also has been featured on "The MacNeil/Lehrer NewsHour" on PBS. Margulies's collection of *Houston Post* cartoons, My Husband Is Not a Wimp, was released in the fall of 1988. In his foreword, *Houston Post* editor Lynn Ashby says, "It is now a badge of honor to be humiliated by a Jimmy Margulies cartoon."

Kevin Kallaugher (better known as KAL) was born in Connecticut but lived and worked for eleven years in Great Britain as a successful editorial cartoonist before returning to the U.S. and his job on *The Baltimore Sun*. He can lay claim to the unique honor of being an editorial cartoonist for three major publications. Besides his usual five cartoons for *The Baltimore Sun,* he does one for *The Economist* magazine of London and then one more for the *International Herald Tribune*, based in Paris.

Before he became a sought-after artist, he survived by doing caricatures of tourists in Brighton Beach and in Trafalgar Square. KAL says that "in the U.S., the editorial cartoonist is in a more exalted position. He is usually the chief satirist in the city—a superstar of sorts. His main competition is Johnny Carson." In England, however, satire is accepted as an everyday part of life, so the focus of attention is not on the editorial cartoonist. In fact, in Great Britain political cartoons are not confined merely to the editorial pages.

KAL feels that political cartoonists must always recognize the sensibilities of their readers. "You can't tick them off so much that they're not going to bother looking at you anymore. You want to tell them your point of view in a way that engages them, not just tell them they're jerks."

Of his art, he says, "You have a lot of responsibility. You're taken bloody seriously. When you do something local, the impact is massive. . . . You only have their attention for five or ten seconds, unlike an editorial column, where people have to decide to read it and invest the time. Political cartoons are the

most accessible form of editorial. Everybody's going to take a chance they might laugh. . . . The idea is not to make them believe you, but to provoke their thoughts and make the democratic process work.''

Strategic Semantics

A clone is a clone is a clone

Jerry Robinson has done about everything there is to do as a cartoonist. First of all, he created the Joker, the world's first comic-book super-villain, while working on the Batman strip at age . . . (are you ready for this?) . . . eighteen. Since then he's collected just about every award that a cartoonist can get, including Best Syndicated Panel, Best Comic Book Artist and others too numerous to mention. He is the creator and artist responsible for Life With Robinson, an internationally syndicated, satirical political cartoon, a few examples of which you see reprinted here.

He's also an author, having written *The Comics: An Illustrated History of Comic Strip Art, The 1970s: Best Political Cartoons of the Decade* and a biography, *Skippy and Percy Crosby*. Robinson also teaches and lectures, and he's a frequent guest speaker at colleges all over America and on TV. He's had cartoon exhibitions in Europe and he's also president and editorial director of the Cartoonists & Writers Syndicate, which he (of course) founded in 1977. How does the man ever have time to draw? And as well as he does?

Robinson confesses that he gets literally thousands of submissions every year. He can immediately eliminate about ninety percent of them right off the bat because of their lack of professionalism, their imitative quality or their inability to graphically depict whatever concept they're trying to sell.

"We look for originality first," Robinson says, "in style and concept. Of course the concept is the most important thing; we look down the long road and assess it on the grounds of good graphic execution and viability. This business is highly competitive so the last thing we are interested in is another version of Peanuts, Doonesbury or Garfield. We look for something offbeat that we can get behind and sell enthusiastically. We have to deal with the editors at the

Generalizations

The Day After the New Hampshire Primary

various newspapers and they're astute people, so the power of the strip is generally its uniqueness."

He adds that "sometimes we'll gamble with somebody who's a little raw; the submissions don't have to be totally slick. If we sense some real ability we'll take a chance and help them to develop."

So, if you've the artistic ability, the humor, the political perspicacity, the awareness and, most of all, the passion to be an editorial cartoonist, take the advice of these seasoned professionals to heart—grab your pens (see weapons) and go for it. We need people out there who can help us to laugh at life, to puncture pomposity, to ridicule the wrongdoers, ferret out the phonies, slam the self-righteous and (I'm sorry, it was a minor seizure of alliteration syndrome) keep our governmental agencies and officials in the proper perspective. A sorely needed service indeed.

# CHILDREN'S BOOKS

In children's books the world is your oyster as far as style is concerned. A major publisher once told me that artists are really appealing to the adult eye because, most often, they are the ones who buy the books for the children. So don't be afraid of using a fairly sophisticated approach that will still appeal to, but not confuse, the young audience. And don't sell kids short; they have a discerning eye for art, and even though they can't always articulate what they like, their gut reaction is usually sound. I've shown children of various ages different pieces of art and asked them which they preferred and, oddly enough, they nearly always chose the better work; they don't know texture or tone or composition yet, but their innate sense informs them.

For many years cartoonists were not considered suitable for children's books but now they dominate the field and rightly so. The artists' humorous slant combined with a carefully nurtured simplicity makes them the perfect choice for instant visual communication with children. The market is broad; it's looking for anything from zany to whimsical to traditional, and if you can do all three then all the better for you. A lot of hiring for children's books is accomplished through other avenues. For example, an art director may spot an artist's panel cartoon, contact the artist and ask him or her to prepare a "dummy," a rough sketchbook integrating pictures and text.

Here's a sample of Frank Daniel's style.

Larry Daste/Evelyne Johnson Associates

Dick Gautier

The alternative route is to woo the art directors at the various publishing houses yourself. Make up a dummy on speculation, based on some classic fairy tale, with one page of color, and send it off to every potential buyer. The sketches can be rough as long as you include a couple of finished drawings, including the color separation. I'd suggest not going beyond forty pages since that seems to be a comfortable compromise (most children's books range from thirty-two to forty-eight pages). And if you can sustain reader interest for that long, you're on your way to impressing those art editors out there.

When you illustrate a children's book, it goes beyond mere drawings; you're also the designer. You take the text and paste it up on the dummy and integrate it with your sketches so that the book has a visual flow, a continuity for the eye. One page might be all illustration with a few words of text and the next page might be all text with a decorative border highlighting some aspect of the story. But the pictures must fit the words on that page. Don't overlap ideas from other pages.

In making a dummy, fold over about sixteen pieces of typewriter paper and staple at the crease. Choose a story, original or otherwise, and go to work on it—the more fanciful and imaginative the better. Art directors are looking for that unusual approach, that elusive stylistic hook that helps to sell the book. You can use any style you please but always keep in mind your target audience. Just don't get obscure or too complicated in your approach.

You most likely will be working in color so knowledge of color separation technique is a must here. We can't really discuss the use of color in this book in any detail but let me just say that, contrary to some artists' view of how to do children's books, I feel that the use of startling colors is not necessary in children's literature. Some of the best, most charming illustrations I've ever seen have been done in muted tones, soft beiges and watery greens. They have, in fact, a soothing restful effect on the reader, so I'd encourage you to experiment. Try to color without the obligatory gaudiness and I think you'll be pleased with the results.

Brian Ajhar

A lot of artists become writers. The text is so minimal, and conceptually the book is primarily visual anyway, so why not create your own? There are a few categories of books: The primarily visual books are aimed at the very young, but then as the age of the child increases, so does the text. Because children's books seem rather basic and simple you might think that they're easy to write, but they're not. First of all, the story must be strong; you can't save a weak (albeit uncomplicated) plot with dazzling illustrations. The text and the pictures must truly complement each other. They are inextricably bound together in the design of the page, more so than with any other form of literature.

A trip to the library and a few hours in the children's section will be an eye-opening experience. You'll see illustrators from Sid Hoff to Shel Silverstein to Tomi Ungerer to Dr. Seuss. All different, all wonderfully well suited to their particular type of book.

Frank Daniel/Evelyne Johnson Associates

Mary Grace Eubank, who was featured in the section on illustration, is a top children's book illustrator, and one glance at her work tells you why. It's clean and appealing. She has an instinct for using just the right amount of distortion in her characters so they at once capture children's attention and amuse them but don't threaten them. Mary Grace has children of her own, but once they're off to school at eight A.M., she changes hats from a June Cleaver housemom to a prolific artist who turns out greeting cards and children's books and comfortably earns a very good living.

Mary Grace made the transition from greeting cards to children's books and she still provides art for "The Children's Television Workshop" and "Sesame Street." She says of her work, "If you gave me an apple, I could draw you an incredibly accurate apple. But that's not all that's required. The creative element was lacking for me. I have been much more inhibited than I would like to be. It's still hard for me to let my lines wiggle."

Benton Mahan, who was also featured earlier, has a very different look for children's books as opposed to his illustrative work. He changes completely for this market. So here are some of his superb illustrations from various books, including *One-Minute Favorite Fairy Tales* by Shari Lewis.

In the section on illustration, I profiled Kathie Abrams, who is a prolific contributor to children's books. Here are some of her illustrations from a variety of books. Notice that these are merely pen-and-ink renderings, and they work beautifully. Color is not always demanded nor fitting for certain stories.

A wonderful exercise for the artist who wants to get into this market is to take a classic fairy tale like *Little Red Riding Hood* and try to find a new way to realize the illustrations, perhaps from the wolf's point of view. Try to make it as arresting and refreshing as you can. Capture the eye of the child, and the adult prospective buyer, with unusual angles, forms and textures.

Be aware that the children's market is broader than fairy tales. You'll find riddle books, joke books (children love telling jokes), puzzle and activity books and many other forms to which you might be drawn. When pitching an original idea, remember that the concept is the thing, so that's where you should put in most of your effort. Book ideas are bought and then the illustrator is hired; the drawings are secondary. It's possible that you could sell a book idea but then a different artist is hired to illustrate it. Maybe your style wasn't right for the book, but what's wrong with that? You've just sold a book. You can illustrate the next one.

Publishers change policies sometimes from day to day; the ones that are busily engaged in producing books for children this year could be turning out self-help books and mysteries the next. To find the names and addresses of current publishers for the younger group, consult the *Literary Market Place,* which should be in your local public library. Another way to get this information is to go to a bookstore. List only the publishers that publish multiple titles every year; asking the clerk in the store will be helpful. Then send out your dummy to all of them and wait. I know this works because this is exactly how I sold my first book. I made the list, sent out letters and followed them up with sketches and a sample chapter. It did the trick for me; it can for you.

John O'Brien/Evelyne Johnson Associates

GREETING CARDS

In the world of greeting cards, the message is definitely the thing. The front of the card has to act as a hook (visual or verbal) to get you interested enough to pick up the card and turn to the punch line inside. It must intrigue you, tug at you, make you want to know how the joke resolves. And more important, surprise you, amuse you and *not disappoint you*. As Max Eastman said in *The Enjoyment of Laughter* (one of the better books of humor analysis, in my opinion), the punch line must contain the "suddenness of the disappointment and the immediacy of the reward"—that is to say, there's nothing worse than a great build that fizzles off into an anticlimactic payoff. The idea is to lead the viewer down the garden path, as it were, toward an ultimately obvious, if not foregone, conclusion and then suddenly provide that "twist," that curve that sends it careening off in another unexpected direction.

In the area of greeting cards, humor is easy in some ways and not in others. First of all, the references, symbols and images are bred into us from childhood, all the clichés, slogans, watchwords and key words are firmly rooted in our minds so any play on them brings immediate recognition; you don't have to give any explanation in order for the audience to catch up with you. Now the downside:

You have to come up with something fresh and new while every other greeting-card humorist, designer and cartoonist is playing around with that same set of phrases and clichés and images.

The important thing about the drawing on the front of the card is that it immediately sets a tone. Our eyes scan the greeting-card display rack and we quickly form a subliminal judgment as to whether this card is right for our needs or our taste. The cartoon should clearly and immediately express whether this card is sentimental, silly, raunchy, reverent, bathetic or banal. (There I go again . . . sorry!)

I spoke at length with Barbara Dale; she and her husband, Jim, the president of an advertising agency, are the creators (she draws, he writes, or sometimes she writes but he never draws) of one of the most successful lines of humorous cards around, called, naturally, Dale Cards. Theirs is truly a mom-and-pop operation and, according to them, they sort of "backed into" the greeting-card business.

Barbara explained it this way: "Jim has always been a writer, I was a ceramicist. We took a romantic holiday together when our baby was just a year old. We started talking about the baby (what else do you do at a romantic dinner?) and I mentioned that I had a funny idea for a greeting card for new mothers. Jim liked the idea and started writing others down on his napkin. We ended up with ten or twelve of what we thought were pretty good card ideas . . . and it was fun. This was back in 1979—all that was available in the card stores was the Hallmark sentimental stuff and those long thin studio cards, and some of those were rather boorish, you know—conventioneers' humor.

"I decided to go to a little printing place and have a few Xeroxes of our cards made up to send to our friends. On my way out, clutching my shoe box full of cards, I ran into a friend who ran a gift shop. He looked at the cards, liked them and asked if he could place them next to his cash register. We had no envelopes or anything, it was just folded-over Xerox paper. A month later the cards were all sold and he wanted more.

"After getting some nice reactions from a few other local card shops, Jim and I decided to put up some money and have them printed the 'right' way. We didn't think that our humor, which is on the edge, would have a mass market appeal but we were proven wrong. They sold . . . and very well.

"Our next step was to hire sales reps to handle our cards for other outlying cities. Our first cards were delivered in used Huggies boxes, left over from the baby (who really started the whole thing). After that we started visiting the New York Stationery Show to show our wares and the owners of Recycled Paper, which is the largest alternative card company around, found us, signed us and bought our company. Since then we've been working with Recycled and Carol Wilson Fine Arts. We do the creating, and they do all the rest of it, including the distribution, handling and licensing of mugs, stationery and all the other ancillary markets."

I asked her about the new people who are trying to get into the business and Barbara had this to say: "Those opportunities are still out there. You can do it inexpensively, but you have to have honesty; you can always get something printed up fairly inexpensively, and you can get feedback by placing them in gift shops and stores. But what most people tend to do is jump into the thing before they're sure they have a good product. There's no reason to have a mediocre product; if you go into it with a mediocre product you'll probably lose your money."

And what about their technique for always coming up with fresh gags? After a moment Barbara replied, "We generally start with a category like birthdays or whatever . . . We use free association. Or we say to ourselves—what kind of birthday card would I like to get? Or use different people that you know; the birthday card that each person you know would like to receive would represent a different point of view. What would they send me or what would I send them? If I send one to Aunt Ethel, I have to think what she would enjoy or what I'd like to say to her. What would make her laugh?

"And once you have something on the page, you can work with it. There's nothing that's ever too horrible or awful to put down on paper. If something has no hope then throw it away. Be ruthless, don't waste your time. The most important thing is listening to your heart. Does this make me laugh? Does it make my friends laugh? That's how we go about it."

Greeting cards, like panel cartoons, fall into three basic categories: the totally visual; the combination of visual and verbal humor, which are symbiotically dependent upon one another; and the third kind, which is merely verbal (in this case, however, the cartoonist might illustrate the cover of the card anyway to act as that visual hook to attract the fickle browser).

Then there's a new, fourth type of card that has recently reared its head in the marketplace and that is the single-panel cartoon that wasn't actually designed for the greeting-card market but artists like Gary Larson or Steve Phillips have been clever enough to work backwards from the cartoon so that it applies to some sort of greeting. Here are a couple of examples.

You can see that the jokes work independently on the front. The inside is merely an addendum so that it qualifies as a greeting card.

Mary Grace Eubank, who designs cards for Hallmark, isn't sure but in 1982 she thinks she illustrated almost 500 greeting cards. She works fast (obviously): "I can draw three to five studio cards in a day and I knew that would be to my advantage." But she works about ten hours a day in order to meet those obligations. She had been designing gift-wraps for a few years when Drawing Board Greeting Cards, a Dallas firm, asked her to work for them, and within a year she was one of their top staff designers.

Here are a couple of examples of the first type of card I mentioned—the setup is on the front and the punch is on the inside.

What the creators have done is establish a seemingly sweet and genuine sentiment (you know there's a joke coming because the art sets a tone) but then it deals its devastating blow on the inside. It's a game; readers understand that they're being set up but since they can't think of the punch they read on, or maybe they outguess you with a better punch line, in which case disappointment sets in and they simply don't buy the card.

The Dales, Jim and Barbara, are terrific at the inside payoff. They always manage to come up with something totally unanticipated and funny.

Then there's the visual setup, the picture so strange that you can't possibly imagine how it could relate to a holiday much less any sentiment. But then as you peek at the second half of the card, you are surprised and delighted. Here are a couple of prime examples of this by a wonderfully weird artist named Whitlark.

Incidentally, all cards don't have to be hysterically funny—very few are, in fact. There is a definite need for the gently whimsical card since everyone doesn't have a bizarre sense of humor. Kathie Abrams, whose illustrations you enjoyed earlier, is a very successful greeting-card artist who doesn't go for the full-out joke. She provides a kinder, gentler kind of card, like this one.

Also, some cards prove to be quite successful with a fairly straight sentiment but the infectiously charming cartoon on the outside takes the edge off the bathos—like this Sandra Boynton card.

Boynton's humor is quite remarkable because in spite of its gentleness, it's still funny. The drawings are extremely simple yet richly individual; I think that's advantageous, to be able to spot a style easily on a card rack. I believe that there's a soothing sense of certainty (based on the consistent quality of their work) that I feel when I see familiar artwork on a card rack. Much like walking into a restaurant and seeing the same maître d', who knows you, or like buying a suit from the same guy over and over again, there's a sense of continuity that appeals to us.

Here are a couple more Boyntons that capture that charming whimsical quality.

The kind of gag card that is strictly verbal is one where if you deleted the cover drawing, the joke would still work. The cover just wouldn't be as eye-catching and you might not pick up the card, so you might as well go for the visual, but it's not necessary to the humor. Here's another card of that variety by the Dales.

Then there are cards that are just funny for the sake of being funny. They don't say "I love you" or "Happy" anything. You just send them to give someone you're fond of a good laugh. Here's a card by Steve Phillips that falls into that category.

And then there are cards that have no message inside with simply a funny drawing on the front. Sometimes these are big sellers because it allows you to tailor-make your message.

And then there are cards that have nothing to do with love or the holidays or anything. They're just supportive, like this one.

But how do we come up with these gags? How do we find that surprising twist that will amuse? First of all, I'd suggest starting with a little list making—the holidays and special event days, for instance,

New Year's	**Memorial Day**
Groundhog Day	**Flag Day**
Lincoln's Birthday	**Father's Day**
Valentine's Day	**Independence Day (4th of July)**
Washington's Birthday	**Yom Kippur**
Saint Patrick's Day	**Columbus Day**
Daylight Saving Begins	**Veterans Day**
Good Friday	**Thanksgiving**
Passover	**Hanukkah**
Easter Sunday	**Christmas**
Mother's Day	

(I know Saint Swithin's Day fits in there somewhere.)

Beyond this list there are a number of other special events, like BIRTHDAYS, ANNIVERSARIES, GRADUATION, HOUSEWARMING, the BIRTH OF A BABY, a PROMOTION, a NEW JOB and a whole mess of cards regarding LOVE, FRIENDSHIP, THANK YOU, etc., etc., etc. Since the list is endless, I don't really have room for it here.

Now, under each holiday or special event or sentiment make yourself a sub-list of words, images and clichés associated with that particular day or event. For instance . . .

CHRISTMAS

TREES, GIFTS, SANTA, REINDEER, ELVES, MRS. CLAUS, YULE LOGS, SNOW, CHILDREN . . . (I'm intentionally avoiding the original religious meaning because obviously it doesn't lend itself to the cartoon style). Do a sort of free-association word test as one image or word leads to another. It doesn't matter if the list comes out to a hundred or more, eventually you'll be grateful for them . . . TINSEL, MISTLETOE, ROOFTOPS, SANTA'S COOKIES, NORTH POLE, GINGERBREAD MEN, A TIE FOR DAD, SCROOGE, FIREPLACES, TINY TIM, TURKEY, RELATIVES OVER, DECORATING THE TREE, SELECTING THE TREE, SUGARPLUMS, TOY SOLDIERS, 'TWAS THE NIGHT BEFORE XMAS, etc. (you can use almost any line from this well-known poem), XMAS CAROLS . . . with a sub-subheading including "Silent Night," "It Came upon a Midnight Clear," etc. . . . BELLS, SLEIGHS, SKATING, RUDOLPH, DANCER, PRANCER, etc., . . . and ad infinitum.

Then scan the list or sit at your drawing board and doodle until something pops out at you. How about something about SANTA'S COOKIES? Maybe instead of a simple plate of cookies it could be a sumptuous feast laid out with a note that says: *For Santa.* Open up the card and it says: "Is bribery really in the Christmas spirit?" Or how about SELECTING THE TREE. Is there something in an image of a giant redwood sticking out of a car or hauling it? Or do you see the tree sticking out of the top of a small cottage? The front could read: "This year

I got you a tree the size of my love." And inside, where we see the illustration, it could say: "But how the heck do I get it into the house?"

Do you get the idea? Establish a mundane premise, one that we've been exposed to a hundred times, and then carry it to a ridiculous extreme. That was the formula for the TREE and SANTA'S COOKIES. Carrying the idea just one step too far until, we hope, it becomes funny.

I had a thought when I was writing this list. I ran across Daylight Saving Time in the calendar—what a perfect opportunity to send someone you love a card . . . because it's a non-reason it becomes humorous. You could bend the idea backward slightly by saying something like: "Happy Daylight Saving Time," and on the inside: "I like it. The nights are longer." It has a lascivious ring but nonetheless it could be a good card. Or you could turn it the other way around, assuming that the lovers are separated: "I miss you more during Daylight Saving Time" . . . (open the card) "The nights are even longer when we're apart." Not funny but sweet and it could be another card out there for you. I also was thinking about *The Night Before Christmas* and the line that goes "I tore open the shutters and threw up . . . the sash" keeps nagging at me. There has to be a joke there somewhere.

That's the kind of crazy thinking to go for. Run that list through your head over and over again until those silly twists and turns start popping out at you.

Start taking the usual and turning it into the unusual; find that last-minute turn that sends the cliché scurrying off in another direction; take the expected and turn it into the unexpected.

Here's a card by Sandra Boynton that simply deals with the word "Congratulations" and yet she finds a way to extract humor from it.

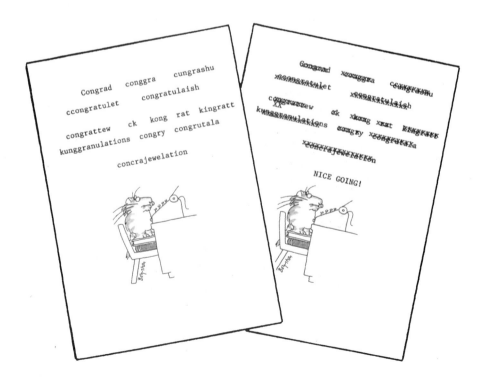

Here's a simple device that's very effective. Sometimes you might want to think very straight and sincere initially even if you don't know where it's going—in other words, don't have a punch line in mind—and then suddenly surprise yourself as you come at it from a different direction.

Okay, now look at the front of this card and write a punch (or punches) for the inside.

THIS BIRTHDAY CHICKEN is very sad. She was going to peck out HAPPY BIRTHDAY TO YOU on a little toy piano, but the little toy piano broke.

Now what did you come up with?

And she
only
had enough
scratch
for this
card.

Now you see what the artist used, so whatever you came up with might be a fresh idea for a card. Go to your card shop and try to guess the punch lines on the inside. If you're right, forget it, it's been done; but if not, you've written yourself a new card. And there's nothing wrong with stealing setups; just ignore their punch lines. It's not plagiarism—it's a wonderful exercise to get your funny juices flowing. It'll put your head in the right place for this part of the business.

Before I close this chapter, just let me say that everyone has strengths and weaknesses and it's only the smart ones who can admit what those weaknesses are. This is, after all, a book about drawing, the creating of gags is peripheral. Maybe you are not a gag writer, but that's okay, maybe you are a brilliant illustrator. So you draw and get someone else to think up the gags. There's a reason why most of the comedy written in movies and on television is written by duos or groups of writers. It's an opportunity to bounce things around for reaction, and it creates a healthy, silly atmosphere. If writing is not your métier, find a partner—you draw, he or she comedes. A marriage made for the greeting-card business.

NIMATION

I have never worked in the field of animation per se. Of course, like all budding artists I tried the experiment with the riffling pages and watched the little stick figure move in a primitive way. So I'm no animation maven; however, I have worked for years doing voices for several cartoon characters—from Serpentor the Evil Cobra Warlord in GI Joe to Spike in Spike and Tyke, the Transformers and a list too long and boring to go into. The point is that I've learned how animation works and I've become friendly with many animators over the years.

The one fact that keeps reasserting itself of late is that the animation business is thriving. There's an incredible amount of activity both here and overseas and the demand for artists who do animation has never been keener. It's an animation renaissance much like the stand-up comedy renaissance of a few years ago. I think it's a combination of several factors: In motion pictures, there's a dearth of G-rated films to which parents can take their children; television (even with its limited animation) is finding more and more outlets for cartoons due to cable and videos; and the producers have discovered that there's an eternal life to animated films and shorts. I think it's safe to say that fifty or one hundred years from now, some child will be watching *Snow White* or *Yogi Bear* somewhere. The thing that helps to make cartoons timeless is that their styles don't change with the times to a great extent; they aren't trendy in their clothing and hairstyles. Only the drawing styles change and even then we accept them as old friends. There's really been no better time to get into the animation business than right now. In his excellent book *Cartoon Animation: Introduction to a Career,* Milton Gray says: "Employment in animation is presently booming in Los Angeles. New people are being absorbed into the industry at a record rate, and the present high level of employment is likely to continue for at least several more years . . . the studios are searching for many more qualified artists. . . . The hope is that more of the new cartoon films in production will be aimed at broader, more adult audiences."

To be an animator you have to love to draw, to draw the human body in motion and to draw the face in a wide range of expressions. You have to love to draw with that sense of visual exaggeration that makes inanimate cels come alive and burst with personality and cartoon charisma. Yes, cartoon charisma . . . Tell me Bugs Bunny or Tom & Jerry or Donald Duck are not charismatic characters. They couldn't have survived all these years without that slightly off-base personality and appealing combination of flaws and quirks that made them the superstars they are—and will continue to be with each succeeding generation.

I spoke with Lance Falk, one of Hanna-Barbera's top animators for seven years, who came into the business through a rather unconventional back door. He's been doing character design (or "models" as they're known in the industry) and has worked in many different capacities. He had art in high school, but no formal training after that. I asked him how he got started in this business. Falk replied: "I was about twenty-three years old, and I was working in the stockroom, so I had sort of an inside track. I heard they were working on 'Jonny Quest.' Well, that was my favorite show when I was a kid. I tried writing scripts. I tried all sorts of things to no avail but then I heard they were hiring a cleanup artist on 'Jonny Quest.' Models are character designs, cleanup is taking rough drawings that other people have already done and putting a fine line on them almost like an inker. Cleanup also consists of turning the character in different positions, sideways if the figure was drawn in a front view. So there is a bit of creativity involved. I heard they needed a cleanup man, so I did research. I took the characters (the roughs) home and started to clean them up. It took me all weekend; I did them and redid them. I missed a lot of parties and movies that weekend but it was worth it. I worked on them until I got them perfect. I walked in Monday morning and submitted them to the supervisor of the show. He resisted at first but when he saw the work, he changed his attitude and hired me on the spot. The nice P.S. is that I also got paid for the portfolio, retroactively for the cleanup work that I had done. From there I've moved into other, more creative areas and I like what I do."

The T-shirt design on the next page was created by Lance for a "Twisted-Disney" party, sort of a "What if a Grateful Dead fan were obsessed with a certain musical revue at the Magic Kingdom?"

I asked Lance about the new people getting into the business. He said: "I used to judge portfolios; a portfolio could consist of cleanups, as well as new characters. Show that you have line ability, which would double or triple your chances of being hired—that is, if you can actually create new original stuff. We look for a versatile person, and we like people who do a lot of things adequately and professionally. I'm not enormously skilled in any one area but I'm competent in about six or seven different styles. That's kept me here. There are periods of layoff; we are generally compartmentalized but we are asked to fill in here and there. In the model department, we use people who do rough drawings and cleanup. And, as far as animation pencil videos are concerned, they're a luxury, not a necessity."

A lot of the artists are asked to draw up model sheets, which are sketches of the character in all poses, attitudes and expressions. This would be a good addition to your portfolio.

Hanna-Barbera®

To get the real scoop on how an animated production gets from the script to the screen, follow along with Hanna-Barbera Productions' superstar Yogi Bear as he illustrates the steps.

1 Scriptwriting/Models—Yogi the writer works on a script containing dialogue, screen directions and sound effects cues. An artist then draws models of all the characters in a variety of poses.

2 Storyboards—Yogi demonstrates how an artist uses the finished script and models to create a storyboard, a comic strip "blueprint" version of the script with dialogue and directions noted beneath each drawing.

3 Layout—Utilizing the storyboards, layout artist Yogi designs production-size backgrounds, props and costumes for each scene. He also stages each scene, noting positioning and action poses for each character.

4 Animation—Yogi the animator makes key drawings of the characters in action. Hanna-Barbera's assistant animators complete the "in-between" drawings that make the characters move from one point to another.

7 Animation Checking—Now posing as a checker, Yogi reviews the animation and layout art work, ensuring that all drawings are completed in sequence and that characters' mouth movements are correctly matched to the dialogue.

10 Cel Painting—Guided by color-coded models of the characters, Yogi the painter chooses from Hanna-Barbera's palette of more than 350 different colors to paint on the underside of each photocopied cel.

11 Camera Work—Following instructions written on the exposure sheets, camera operator Yogi photographs the animation and backgrounds, exposing one frame at a time. It takes 24 frames to create a single second of film.

12 Editing—After the film is developed, Yogi the editor synchronizes the dialogue to the picture, adding the appropriate music and sound effects on separate tracks and detailing the final timing.

Then I went in to talk to the men themselves. Bill Hanna and Joe Barbera, two of the true giants of animation, co-creators of Tom & Jerry, Yogi Bear, The Flintstones, Scooby-Doo, the Jetsons, etc., etc., etc. They both spoke candidly with me regarding the state of animation today and how they feel a newcomer can get into the business.

Recording—While the storyboard is prepared, Yogi joins other voice actors at the Hanna-Barbera recording studio where their reading of the script is captured on tape.

Track Reading—Here, Yogi listens to the voice recording, measuring and writing down every vowel and consonant on "exposure sheets" where each space corresponds to a frame of film. The animator uses this visual record of dialogue to synchronize action with sound.

Background Painting—In the role of background artist, Yogi follows the penciled layout drawings to complete the color and detail for every landscape or interior setting.

Photocopying—Yogi shows how the animators' original drawings are carefully photocopied, or inked, onto clear acetate sheets or cels.

Completion—Yogi now has the final print which combines all the elements, including picture, dialogue, sound effects and music cues, and brings the Hanna-Barbera cartoon to life.

Enjoyment—The final master tape is sent to a broadcast system for televising, and Yogi can sit back to enjoy the fruit (and popcorn) of his labor.

Bill Hanna feels that "the standards are so much higher now, to get into the business. You have to be an accomplished artist. The requirements have risen. The schools that teach animation and background painting are attracting fine artists. Cal Arts, here in Los Angeles, is one of the finest schools, the people that are coming out of there are getting jobs. Those who come out of Cal Arts don't start as in-betweeners, they are animators. Some are effects animators, some are character animators, some do backgrounds but they do well enough to get by doing simple animation. However, if someone were to come in with a portfolio or a pencil test that qualified, he or she would be hired. There's a great need for qualified people right now. There are more animated cartoons in production right now than in the history of the industry. If they are good draftsmen, if they have a good portfolio, we'd put them into a training program, start them at the bottom and let them work their way up into becoming a top animator. Their portfolio should show off their ability as an artist—drawings, water color, oils. We'll take a look and decide what their strengths are, whether they belong in backgrounds, characters or whatever. Then we can move them around until we find the area in which they seem to be strongest. So toss everything out and let us judge as to whether they're qualified and in what area.

"And it's not necessary to live in the immediate area. If an artist lives out of town, they could send in a portfolio and if we liked it, yes, we would consider employing them. We have done that in the past and we've done it with writers. They should send their artwork in; it will be judged on that, not the appearance or location of the person. There is a storyboard artist who lives in Minnesota and faxes the material right here to Hanna-Barbera from his home."

Joe Barbera had a slightly different view of the situation. "I personally feel that if you can draw, even a little, it will help you in this business. I myself am not a trained artist. I took no classes. I worked in a bank, which I hated, I didn't belong there, I can't add. They promoted me to being a tax man, so in desperation I turned to what I loved—drawing cartoons. I tried to sell them to magazines. After a while I finally sold one and then I got a job at Max Fleischer animation studios. I hated that, too. I was there four days but I learned about animation. I was selling more cartoons to magazines when I ran into a fraternity brother and he sent me to a cartoon studio. I got the job because of my magazine cartoon work. That started my career in the animation business.

"You don't have to be a great artist to be an animator—you have to understand movement. You have to know attitudes, movement, feeling. That's what I look for in a portfolio. Put in what you do, it'll make it or not. Whenever you can take a class of any kind, take it. If you want to animate, you can do a scene on your own. Take a stick figure and create a scene for yourself. You have to be observant; notice the way people move, the way things move, what water does when it splashes.

"It's observation, desire, persistence. Don't let anybody talk you out of it—because they need people today. There's more animation being done today than ever. Everywhere—Spain, France. We don't have enough good people. Last week we were looking for layout men; there were none available. . . . We don't take on apprentices, although I feel we need them. I started classes here. They went for over three years but the studio didn't take advantage of the people from the class. They hired a few, who turned out thirteen feet of animation a week but when the studio wanted forty, they were laid off. Now we ship the stuff to Taipei so we don't have the control we used to have. Disney uses our studio in Taipei, and we also have one in the Philippines. They do Xeroxing of the cels and the painting; we even have in-betweeners there. It's never as good as doing everything in-house but it's getting better. If all those foreign companies said we don't want to do it anymore, we'd be out of business. We don't have it here. We need qualified people."

When I was attending Hamilton High School in Los Angeles, my archrival in the cartoon drawing area (and good friend) was Art Leonardi. After graduation we went our separate ways. I pursued the theater while Art chased cartooning and animation. He caught it—and very successfully. Art has directed theatrical shorts for Warner Brothers, including *The Pink Panther* and *The Ant and the Aardvark*. As well as writing and directing TV series, he did titles for Blake Edwards's *The Revenge of the Pink Panther* and *The Trail of the Pink Panther* and recently won an Emmy for his direction of a Tiny Toons segment entitled "The Anvil Chorus." As of this writing, he's directing and producing *Shelley Duvall's Bedtime Stories* at Universal Cartoon Studios. This is a caricature of Art courtesy of Robert Camargo.

When Art left high school, I learned over lunch at the commissary, he got a job right away as a comic-book cartoonist. He says: "I was mostly fixing up other artists' work but it was okay; I was about eighteen or nineteen years old and making a living as a cartoonist. One night one of my bosses asked me to go bowling and between games I was doing some sketching. My boss's brother saw what I was doing and hired me on the spot to work with him as an animator at Warner Brothers. Of course, I started at the bottom. I was an in-betweener, then I pushed to be an assistant. Then Friz Freleng asked me to be his assistant and I ended up working there for twenty-four years. I had approached Bill Hanna and Joe Barbera years before and was summarily rejected, so it was odd going to work for them a few years later in my capacity as full-fledged animator and producer.

BUSTERING WITH PRIDE!

ART LEONARDI

"In this business, being a good artist is not enough. You can see a great artist whom you'd like to bring in and teach him animation from the ground up. But remember, he has to understand film technique as well; he has to be able to draw up a storyboard and have it make 'film sense.' Artists who want to go into animation should pick up some books and read about it, start learning the process. Sometimes we compartmentalize—he does the backgrounds, she animates—but if you can do it all, it's an advantage.

"This new project, *Shelley Duvall's Bedtime Stories,* is a real challenge. We're doing six books and we have to stick to the visual style of each book. Our writer has to not only supplement the dialogue with new lines, but find subplots to flesh out the story *plus* keep all of the original dialogue intact. As I say, it's a challenge."

Gabor Csupo (pronounced *Chu-po*) is one half of the team of Klasky-Csupo, Inc. The Klasky is his wife, Arlene, a talented graphic designer whom he met in Stockholm in the late seventies. Gabor was an active and successful animator in his native Hungary but he fled the country in 1975 by way of a harrowing two-and-a-half-hour walk though a darkened railway tunnel to Austria and freedom. He worked in Stockholm for a few years until he met Arlene and together they relocated to Southern California and formed Klasky-Csupo, Inc. The company caught fire immediately because of its unusual approach to animation design and its uncompromising devotion to quality.

Csupo says: "I went to an art school. I was always interested in film and art, so the perfect thing for me was animation, to bring film and art together.

A C T I O N   P O S E S

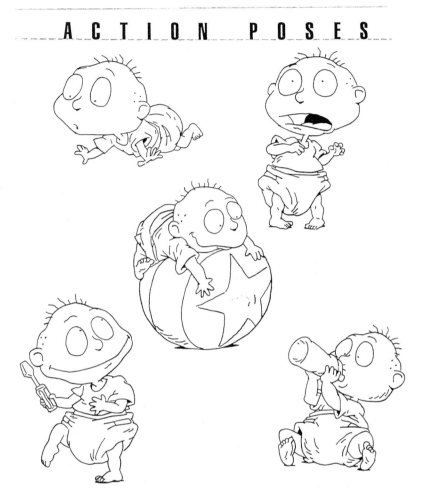

But the schools didn't teach animation. . . . The reason I left the country is that I felt you couldn't say exactly what you wanted to say. In the early seventies (it's different now, of course) I saw very talented directors turning in very good storyboards, but after going through the hierarchy and the censors, they had to change the endings and they were suffering.

"When I came here with my wife, I had no contacts. I tried to go to work at the smaller independent animation studios but when they asked to see my reel, I didn't know what that was. I had no portfolio, nothing. In Europe they hire you based on what school you attended; here they want to see your reel. I finally got a job at Hanna-Barbera. I worked there for six to eight months but then they laid off a lot of people and I was laid off, too. I started to get some free-lance work because I now had a local reference with Hanna-Barbera, and then my wife, who had started a small film graphics company with two other partners, suggested we combine our talents. With her background in design and my background as a traditional animator, it was a perfect combination.

"We got started getting jobs immediately. One job we got—a local TV station wanted something in computer animation but couldn't afford it so they came to us. I said, 'I'll fake it for you.' So we animated like the computer which imitates us.

"James Brooks, the noted television writer/producer, came to us and asked us to do a few cartoon pieces to break up the sketches on *The Tracey Ullman Show,* and next thing you know we were doing *The Simpsons* full-time. This was after we were in the business for five years. Then came Rugrats and we're in the planning stages with several more.

"We have a test for new artists or animators who want to come into the business. They take it home, work on it and we look at it and then we decide whether we think they can do the job. We don't ask for reels or portfolios. A reel is helpful, no doubt about it, but it's not necessary.

"I like to mix in very talented painters or designers—those are the kinds of people I like to get into our organization. When we find people like that, we bring them in and teach them animation."

P M S C O L O R S

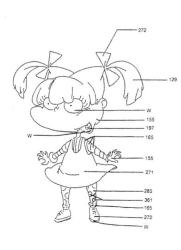

Well, there you are—several different but fascinating stories, demonstrating a variety of paths taken to achieve the same goal: success in the world of animation. I think what we've learned is that you must love the art of animation enough to sacrifice for it, to work hard at it. You must love the human form, anatomy, exaggeration, physical hyperbole—you must love it all and still be able to laugh at it, and what's more, be able to make other people laugh at it.

We didn't find any absolute answers here; some recommended schooling while others have risen to the top of the industry by the sheer dint of talent and persistence. If this is what you really want, don't let anyone deter you. Go after it with a vengeance and don't slow down until you achieve the heights that you feel you deserve.

CLOSING REMARKS

As I bring yet another book to an uncertain close, I'm trying to reassess what was potentially learned here. It's ultimately up to you to apply any clues, tips, hints, advice, instruction or whatever you've gotten from my efforts. I hope that some of it rubbed off—if nothing else a burning desire to work at it, to know that you can help to realize your dreams sitting in a small apartment kitchen late at night armed with nothing but a pen, paper, postage and perseverance. (I know, I know, get off my case!)

But it can be done. Like the top rock groups that started rehearsing in garages, like the writers carrying soiled manuscripts under their arms, all dreams have to start somewhere. You might as well start now, wherever you are. Grab that pencil and draw. Draw funny. Draw furiously. Draw obsessively . . . but draw!

Your place in this world can often be measured in direct ratio to the amount of effort you put forth, and your passion quotient. Find a dispassionate artist and you'll either find a disenchanted or a lazy one. Let that fire to be an artist ignite your every moment and fill your life with productive and enjoyable years to come.

I'm certain that when this book finally goes to press and I'm physically restrained from making any last-minute additions, revisions or deletions, my mind will suddenly come alive (a little late for that, Dick) with all sorts of other ideas and things that I never got around to saying or suggesting. But then there's always that next book, isn't there? I mean, after all, if there can be a *Rocky V* . . .

Please accept my profound praise and plaudits for putting up with my plodding, perhaps pretentious prose; I prize your paramount patience, perseverance, prudence and penultimate perspicacity . . . plus your purchasing power.

There, I think I finally have it out of my system. . . .

Appendix A

Selected Bibliography

Armstrong, Roger. *How to Draw Comic Strips*. Tustin, California: Foster Art Service, 1990.

Blair, Preston. *Animation*. Tustin, California: Foster Art Service, 1987.

———. *How to Animate Film Cartoons*. Tustin, California: Foster Art Service, 1987.

Crawford, Tad. *Legal Guide for the Visual Artist: The Professional's Handbook*. New York: Hawthorn Books, 1977.

Evarts, Susan. *The Art and Craft of Greeting Cards*. Cincinnati: North Light Books, 1982.

Fleishman, Michael. *Getting Started as a Freelance Illustrator or Designer*. Cincinnati: North Light Books, 1990.

Fogle, James, and Mary E. Forsell. *Comps, Storyboards, and Animatics*. New York: Watson-Guptill, 1989.

Gerberg, Mort. *Cartooning: The Art and the Business*. New York: Morrow Publishing, 1989.

Hess, Stephen, and Milton Kaplan. *The Ungentlemanly Art: A History of American Political Cartoons*. New York: Macmillan, 1975.

Jones, Chuck. *Chuck Amuck: The Life and Times of an Animated Cartoonist*. New York: Farrar, Straus & Giroux, 1989.

Markow, Jack. *Writer's Digest Cartoonist's and Gag Writer's Handbook*. Cincinnati: Writer's Digest, 1967.

Meglin, Nick. *The Art of Humorous Illustration*. New York: Watson-Guptill, 1973.

Ross, Al. *Cartooning Fundamentals*. New York: Stravon Publishing, 1977.

Sandman, Larry, ed. *Guide to Greeting Card Writing*. Cincinnati: Writer's Digest, 1985.

Thomas, Bob. *Walt Disney, The Art of Animation: The Story of the Disney Studio Contribution to a New Art*. New York: Simon and Schuster, 1958.

Westin, Alan F. *Getting Angry Six Times a Week: A Portfolio of Political Cartoons by Fourteen Major Cartoonists*. Boston: Beacon Press, 1979.

Appendix B

Syndicates

Cartoonists & Writers Syndicate
67 Riverside Drive
New York, NY 10024
(212) 362-9256

Creators Syndicate
5777 W. Century Boulevard, #700
Los Angeles, CA 90045
(213) 337-7003

King Features Syndicate
North American Syndicate
235 East 45th Street
New York, NY 10017
(212) 682-5600

Los Angeles Times Syndicate
Times Mirror Square
Los Angeles, CA 90053
(213) 237-7987 or (800) 528-4637

Newspapers Enterprise Association, Inc.
200 Park Avenue
New York, NY 10166
(212) 692-3700 or (800) 221-4816

Tribune Media Services, Inc.
64 East Concord Street
Orlando, FL 32801
(407) 839-5600 or (800) 322-3068

United Feature Syndicate
200 Park Avenue
New York, NY 10166
(212) 692-3700 or (800) 221-4816

Universal Press Syndicate
4900 Main Street
Kansas City, MO 64112
(816) 932-6600

Washington Post Writers Group
1150 15th Street, N.W.
Washington, D.C. 20071
(202) 334-6375

Appendix C

Greeting Card Publishers

Gibson Greetings, Inc.
2100 Section Road
Cincinnati, OH 45237
(513) 841-6600

C. R. Gibson Company
32 Knight Street
Norwalk, CT 06851
(203) 847-4543

Hallmark Cards, Inc.
25th and McGee Trafficway
Kansas City, MO 64108
(816) 274-5111

The Maine Line Company
P.O. Box 947
Rockland, ME 04841
(207) 594-2457 or (800) 624-6363

Paper Moon Graphics
P.O. Box 34672
Los Angeles, CA 90034
(310) 645-8700

Recycled Paper Products
3636 North Broadway
Chicago, IL 60613
(312) 348-6410

Sunrise Publications Inc.
1145 Sunrise Greetings Court
Bloomington, IN 47404
(812) 336-9900

Carol Wilson Fine Arts
3021 NE Broadway
Portland, OR 97232
(503) 281-0780

Appendix D

Animation Studios

Howard Beckerman Animation Inc.
35–38 169th Street
Flushing, NY 11358
(718) 359-0898

Hanna-Barbera Productions Inc.
3400 Cahuenga Boulevard
Hollywood, CA 90068
(213) 851-5000

Klasky-Csupo, Inc.
1258 N. Highland Ave
Hollywood, CA 90038
(213) 463-0145

Walt Disney Studios
500 S. Buena Vista
Burbank, CA 91521
(818) 560-1000

Appendix E

Reference Journals, Publications and Organizations

American Institute of Graphic Arts
1059 Third Avenue
New York, NY 10021
(212) 752-0813

Children's Book Council
568 Broadway, Suite 404
New York, NY 10012
(212) 966-1990

Copyright Office
Library of Congress
Washington, D.C. 20559
(202) 287-9100 or (202) 479-0700 for information

Editor & Publisher Syndicate Directory
11 West 19th Street
New York, NY 10011
(212) 675-4380

Graphic Artists Guild, and the Graphic Artists Guild handbook: *Pricing and Ethical Guidelines*
11 West 20th Street
New York, NY 10011
(212) 463-7730

Greeting Card Association
1350 New York Avenue, N.W., Suite 615
Washington, D.C. 20005
(202) 393-1778

Greeting Card Magazine
309 Fifth Avenue
New York, NY 10016
(212) 679-6677

National Cartoonists Society
157 West 57th Street, Suite 904
New York, NY 10019
(212) 333-7606

Cartoonists Association
PO Box 4203
Grand Central Station
New York, NY 10063-4203
(212) 348-8023

Museum of Cartoon Art
Comly Avenue
Rye Brook, NY 10573
(914) 939-0234

American Illustrator
Watson-Guptill
1515 Broadway
New York, NY 10036
(212) 764-7300

Artist's Market
Writer's Digest Books
F & W Publications
1507 Dana Avenue
Cincinnati, OH 45207
(513) 531-2222

RSVP The Directory of Illustration and Design
PO Box 314
Brooklyn, NY 11205
(718) 857-9267

American Illustration Showcase
Watson-Guptill
American Showcase, Inc.
724 Fifth Avenue
New York, NY 10019-4182
(212) 245-0981

Society of Illustrators
128 East 63rd Street
New York, NY 10003
(212) 838-2560

Index

About the Author

Dick Gautier was drawing cartoons for his high school paper in Los Angeles when he was sixteen, singing with a band when he was seventeen and doing stand-up comedy when he was eighteen. After a stint in the Navy, he plied his trade at the prestigious "hungry i" in San Francisco for a year before traveling to the East Coast, where he performed in all the major supper clubs, including an extended run with Barbra Streisand at the Bonsoir in Greenwich Village. He was tagged at The Blue Angel by Gower Champion to play the title role in the smash Broadway musical *Bye Bye Birdie,* for which he won the Tony and Most Promising Actor nominations.

After two years he returned to Hollywood to star in five TV series, including *Get Smart,* in which he created the memorable role of Hymie, the white-collar robot; and he portrayed a dashing but daffy Robin Hood for Mel Brooks in his *When Things Were Rotten.*

Add to this list guest-starring roles in more then 300 TV shows, such as *Matlock, Murder, She Wrote, Columbo,* and *The Tonight Show,* and starring in a slew of feature films with people like Jane Fonda, Dick Van Dyke, George Segal, Debbie Reynolds, Ann Jillian, James Stewart, etc., etc. He's won awards for his direction of stage productions, *Mass Appeal* and *Cactus Flower* with Nanette Fabray, and he's written and produced motion pictures.

He is the author/illustrator of *The Art of Caricature* and *The Creative Cartoonist* for Perigee Books, and he's just completed a coffee-table book with partner Jim McMullan entitled *Actors as Artists.* He's done just about everything but animal orthodontics, and don't count him out on that yet. No wonder he refers to himself as a "renaissance dilettante."

Of all his accomplishments, Gautier is proudest of the fact that he's never hosted a talk show, or gone public with tales of drug rehabilitation and a dysfunctional family life.

Learn to Draw

with Illustrated Instruction Books from Perigee

By Dick Gautier:

_The Career Cartoonist   0-399-51732-4/$10.95
_The Creative Cartoonist   0-399-51434-1/$11.00
_Drawing and Cartooning 1,001 Caricatures   0-399-51911-4/$11.00
_Drawing and Cartooning 1,001 Faces   0-399-51767-7/$10.95
_Drawing and Cartooning 1,001 Figures in Action   0-399-51859-2/$10.95

By Jack Hamm:

_Cartooning the Head & Figure   0-399-50803-1/$9.00
_Drawing and Cartooning for Laughs   0-399-51634-4/$8.95
_Drawing Scenery: Seascapes and Landscapes   0-399-50806-6/$9.95
_Drawing the Head & Figure   0-399-50791-4/$8.95
_First Lessons in Drawing and Painting   0-399-51478-3/$10.95
_How to Draw Animals   0-399-50802-3/$7.95

By Tony Tallarico:

_Drawing and Cartooning Comics   0-399-51946-7/$9.95
_Drawing and Cartooning Dinosaurs   0-399-51814-2/$7.95
_Drawing and Cartooning Monsters   0-399-51785-5/$7.95
_Drawing and Cartooning Myths, Magic and Legends
                                          0-399-52139-9/$8.95

Also Available:

_The Art of Cartooning *by Jack Markow*   0-399-51626-3/$9.00
_Drawing Animals *by Victor Perard, Gladys Emerson Cook and Joy Postle*
                                          0-399-51390-6/$9.00
_Drawing People *by Victor Perard and Rune Hagman*
                                          0-399-51385-X/$9.00
_Sketching and Drawing for Children *by Genevieve Vaughan-Jackson*
                                          0-399-51619-0/$8.50

Or check above books and send this order form to:
The Berkley Publishing Group
390 Murray Hill Pkwy., Dept. B
East Rutherford, NJ 07073

Bill my: ☐ Visa   ☐ MasterCard   ☐ Amex   expires _____

Card #_____
                                         ($15 minimum)
Signature_____

Please allow 6 weeks for delivery

Or enclosed is my: ☐ check   ☐ money order

Name_____   Book Total $_____

Address_____   Postage & Handling $_____

City_____   Applicable Sales Tax $_____
                                    (NY, NJ, PA, CA, GST Can.)
State/ZIP_____   Total Amount Due $_____

Learn the Art of Calligraphy

by Margaret Shepherd

_Calligraphy Alphabets Made Easy

0-399-51257-8/$10.00

A new concept in learning and improving calligraphy skills, here's a book which presents a new lettering challenge for each day of the year—365 in all.

_Calligraphy Made Easy

0-399-50964-X/$8.95

The art of beautiful lettering in eight easy lessons, by the nation's foremost calligraphy author.

_Margaret Shepherd's Calligraphy Projects

0-399-50908-9/$8.95

A fully illustrated how-to book designed for the beginning or intermediate calligrapher who needs practical advice. The book contains lettering projects, how-to illustrations, and over 100 examples of finished designs.

_Modern Calligraphy Made Easy

0-399-51450-3/$8.95

America's leading author of books about calligraphy introduces a new, streamlined form of lettering that brings the ancient art of beautiful writing into the modern world.